INTERVENTIONS AN

Core concepts in therapy

Series editor: Michael Jacobs

Over the last ten years a significant shift has taken place in the relations between representatives of different schools of therapy. Instead of the competitive and often hostile reactions we once expected from each other, therapists from different points of the spectrum of approaches are much more interested in where they overlap and where they differ. There is a new sense of openness to cross orientation learning.

The Core Concepts in Therapy series compares and contrasts the use of similar terms across a range of the therapeutic models, and seeks to identify where different terms appear to denote similar concepts. Each book is authored by two therapists, each one from a distinctly different orientation; and where possible each one from a different continent, so that an international dimension becomes a feature of this network of ideas.

Each of these short volumes examines a key concept in psychological therapy, setting out comparative positions in a spirit of free and critical enquiry, but without the need to prove one model superior to another. The books are fully referenced and point beyond themselves to the wider literature on each topic.

INTERVENTIONS AND TECHNIQUES

Lynn Seiser
and
Colin Wastell

Open University Press
Buckingham · Philadelphia

Open University Press
Celtic Court
22 Ballmoor
Buckingham
MK18 1XW

email: enquiries@openup.co.uk
world wide web: www.openup.co.uk

and
325 Chestnut Street
Philadelphia, PA 19106, USA

First Published 2002

A catalogue record of this book is available from the British Library

ISBN   0 335 20709 X (pb)   0 335 20710 3 (hb)

Library of Congress Cataloging-in-Publication Data
  Seiser, Lynn, 1950–
    Interventions and techniques / Lynn Seiser & Colin Wastell.
      p. cm. – (Core concepts in therapy)
    Includes bibliographical references (p.) and index.
    ISBN 0-335-20710-3 – ISBN 0-335-20709-X (pbk.)
    1. Psychotherapy. I. Wastell, Colin, 1953– II. Title. III. Series.

  RC480.5 .S4167 2002
  616.89'14–dc21   2001056011

Typeset by Graphicraft Limited, Hong Kong
Printed in Great Britain by The Cromwell Press, Trowbridge

Dedications

I would like to dedicate this, my first, I hope, of many books, to all my teachers as educators, clients, colleagues and psychotherapists who taught me the craft and the art of psychotherapy through their knowledge, wisdom, patience and compassion. I also dedicate this work, in humble thanks, to my family and friends for teaching me that the core concept in life, as in psychotherapy, is to learn to let my love out and to learn to let their love in.

Lynn Seiser, PhD, MFCC
Seal Beach, CA, USA, 2001

I dedicate this book to those who will read it in the spirit of the quest to be a growing, developing and maturing therapist. It is to these people that I dedicate the effort that has gone into this work. I wish to thank a number of people. Over the years I have learnt many things from the therapist colleagues with whom I have practiced. To them my sincere thanks. To those clients who have entrusted me with some part of their life in the hope that what I do will make a difference, please accept my humble gratitude. And to my wife, Paula, and sons, Scott and Michael, thank you for your love, support and admiration. It is these things which keep me alive in so many ways.

Colin A. Wastell, PhD, MAPS
Sydney, NSW, Australia, 2001

Contents

Series editor's preface

A major aspect of intellectual and cultural life in the twentieth century has been the study of psychology – present of course for many centuries in practical form and expression in the wisdom and insight to be found in spirituality, in literature and in the dramatic arts, as well as in arts of healing and guidance, both in the East and West. In parallel with the deepening interest in the inner processes of character and relationships in the novel and theatre in the nineteenth century, psychiatry reformulated its understanding of the human mind, and encouraged, in those brave enough to challenge the myths of mental illness, new methods of exploration of psychological processes.

The second half of the twentieth century in particular witnessed an explosion of interest both in theories about personality, psychological development, cognition and behaviour, as well as in the practice of therapy, or perhaps more accurately, the therapies. It also saw, as is not uncommon in any intellectual discipline, battles between theories and therapists of different persuasions, particularly between psychoanalysis and behavioural psychology, and each in turn with humanistic and transpersonal therapies, as well as within the major schools themselves. Such arguments are not surprising, and indeed objectively can be seen as healthy – potentially promoting greater precision in research, alternative approaches to apparently intractable problems, and deeper understanding of the wellsprings of human thought, emotion and behaviour. It is nonetheless disturbing that for many decades there was such a degree of sniping and entrenchment of positions from therapists who should have been able to look more closely at their own responses and rivalries.

It is as if diplomats had ignored their skills and knowledge and resorted in their dealings with each other to gun slinging.

The psychotherapeutic enterprise has also been an international one. There were a large number of centres of innovation, even at the beginning – Paris, Moscow, Vienna, Berlin, Zurich, London, Boston USA – and soon Edinburgh, Rome, New York, Chicago and California saw the development of different theories and therapeutic practice. Geographical location has added to the richness of the discipline, particularly identifying cultural and social differences, and widening the psychological debate to include, at least in some instances, sociological and political dimensions.

The question has to be asked – given the separate developments due to location, research interests, personal differences, and splits between the within traditions – whether what has sometimes been called 'psycho-babble' is indeed a welter of different languages describing the same phenomena through the particular jargon and theorizing of the various psychotherapeutic schools. Or are there genuine differences, which may lead sometimes to the conclusion that one school has got it right, while another has therefore got it wrong; or that there are 'horses for courses'; or, according to the Dodo principle, that 'all shall have prizes'?

The latter part of the twentieth century saw some rapprochement between the different approaches to the theory and practice of psychotherapy (and counselling), often due to the external pressures towards organizing the profession responsibly and to the high standards demanded of it by health care by the public and by the state. It is out of this budding rapprochement that there came the motivation for this series, in which a number of key concepts that lie at the heart of the psychotherapies can be compared and contrasted across the board. Some of the terms used in different traditions may prove to represent identical concepts; others may look similar, but in fact highlight quite different emphases, which may or may not prove useful to those who practise from a different perspective; other terms, apparently identical, may prove to mean something completely different in two or more schools of psychotherapy.

In order to carry out this project it seemed essential that as many of the psychotherapeutic traditions as possible should be represented in the authorship of the series; and to promote both this, and the spirit of dialogue between traditions, it seemed also desirable that there should be two authors for each book, each one representing, where practicable, different orientations. It was important that the series should be truly international in its approach and therefore in its authorship; and that miracle of late twentieth-century technology, the Internet, proved to be a productive means of finding authors, as well as a remarkably efficient method of communicating, in the cases of some pairs of authors, halfway across the world.

This series therefore represents, in a new millennium, an extremely exciting development, one which as series editor I have found more and more enthralling as I have eavesdropped on the drafts shuttling back and forth between authors. Here, for the first time, the reader will find all the major concepts of all the principal schools of psychotherapy and counselling (and not a few minor ones) drawn together so that they may be compared, contrasted, and (it is my hope) above all used – used for the ongoing debate between orientations, but more importantly still, used for the benefit of clients and patients who are not at all interested in partisan positions, but in what works, or in what throws light upon their search for healing and understanding.

Michael Jacobs

CHAPTER 1

Introduction and overview

Two major factors contribute to the success of psychotherapy. The first is the willingness of the client to be open and trusting enough to disclose their pain and their fear, their troubled thoughts and troubling feelings, as well as the courage to make positive changes in their lives in thought, feeling and behaviour. The second factor is the competence of the professional psychotherapist or counsellor. This volume deals directly with this latter factor.

Then there are two particular aspects that contribute to the competence of the therapist. The first is who the psychotherapist is as a person; this is addressed in companion volumes in the series, such as *The Therapist's Use of Self* and *The Therapeutic Environment*. The second important aspect is what the psychotherapist *does* and this aspect is addressed by this volume. Competence as a person comes from personal growth, through therapy and through life experience. It includes acknowledging our connection as equals with those whom we call patients or clients, and with whom we share much by virtue of our common humanity. Competence in the skills of psychotherapeutic interventions and techniques is something that the client is less likely to possess, coming as it does from proper training, practice and supervision.

Psychotherapy is both a craft and an art. The psychotherapist develops the craft through the practice of the specific interventions and techniques, according to the training of the different schools, which are presented in the book. The art comes from the creative process inherent in each of us. However well we learn the craft, it is the way the art is practised, with empathy and compassion, that probably counts for most.

Psychotherapy has also been called a science – that was certainly Freud's dream – and cognitive therapists have employed scientific principles to check the efficacy of their interventions. This art, craft and science of psychotherapy has grown enormously since the start of the twentieth century. The interventions and techniques of psychotherapy have made it possible to talk (depending on orientation) about our childhood, our hopes and our dreams, our thoughts and our feelings, scales of what trouble us most and our life's philosophy. Psychotherapy and counselling (or 'therapy' as we shall generally call these linked disciplines) provide a safe and supportive context in which to explore, to become more aware, to express, to practice alternative ways of being and to change. Western societies accept the help of professionals for mental, emotional and psychological problems. Once considered a demonstration of weakness, sometimes resulting in further shame and guilt, the public now largely considers therapy a positive, safe and healthy alternative. Theories about human cognition, behaviour, emotion and relatedness, examined by psychology, have been operationalized through interventions and techniques that make change not only possible but to a greater extent predictable, and more under conscious choice and control.

It is our sincere effort to give a broad overview of the interventions and techniques employed in the most commonly accepted schools of psychotherapy. The theoretical orientation of the psychotherapist will make a difference in the interactions, interventions and techniques brought into play with the client, and most therapists justify such techniques as being related to the outcome of psychotherapy (see the later companion volume in the series, *Objectives and Outcomes*). In some cases the major differences are largely about emphasis, and some therapies (notably the integrative and eclectic models) shun exclusivity. The main differences between orientations are the emphases placed on the inner versus the interpersonal, understanding versus feelings versus behaviour, past versus present versus future, and growth versus the elimination of problem symptom behaviours.

Interventions and Techniques focuses on specific techniques and interventions that therapists use to produce change. This volume describes, defines and demonstrates the clinical applications of these techniques throughout the diverse approaches to treatment. Some schools of psychotherapy claim not to use techniques, a claim which we examine critically. However, all schools describe a contextual, communication, or interaction model that easily lends itself to classification of techniques or the process of interventions.

This volume assumes the reader possesses some familiarity with the field of psychotherapy and counselling generally, probably with one or two schools of psychotherapy; and enables the reader to explore familiar ideas in the context of other orientations. The book provides sufficient explanation to allow a reader, who is new to a particular school of thought, the ability to understand techniques and interventions used in many schools or orientations of therapy.

Evolution of psychotherapeutic interventions and techniques

Before the twentieth century there was no separate field known as psychotherapy. The behavioural problems of an individual were dealt with within the family, within the community or punitively by whatever criminal justice system existed. The emotional problems of the individual were dealt with by the family, the community and by the church or other faith community.

The twentieth century saw the dawning of a new age, the age of psychotherapy. The beginning of each separate school of psychotherapy, and its particular emphasis in theory and/or practice, has often been by way of reaction to, or growth out of, another school. It is partly this that makes it difficult at times to identify clear differences. Nevertheless, most of the schools of psychotherapy that have developed are still widely practiced and there are at times lively debates between them.

What we call the First Wave evolved from the psychoanalytic tradition that originated with Sigmund Freud at the beginning of the twentieth century, particularly coming to the notice of physicians during the first decade (1900–1910). Psychoanalysis was imported into the United States in 1909 at the invitation of G. Stanley Hall when Freud delivered the Clark lectures. It reflected the European culture and mentality. Its major goal was self-understanding, insight and the uncovering of subjective meanings of symptoms and symbols. From the Victorian era there was a sense of self as internal, rational, secular, hard-working, self-disciplined, frugal, split between genders and secretly sexual and aggressive (Freedheim 1992). The tense, repressed, overworked, humourless, and over intellectualized context presented both the content and the method for early psychoanalytic or psychodynamic interventions and techniques based partly on the medical model, but developed in response to dissatisfaction with imposing solutions on patients. The context was private practice and privately funded. Public facilities left the impression that they were reserved for the grossly dysfunctional and impaired. In the second decade Carl Jung (Pettijohn 1986) broke from his association with Freud to establish analytic psychology, which emphasized the psychological typing of introvert and extrovert, the collective unconscious (racial memory) and universal symbols or mental instincts as archetypes.

What we call the Second Wave is the behaviourist school, which emerged from the psychological researches of John B. Watson (1913). The First World War created a need for psychological services, which in Europe enabled psychoanalysis to flourish; it also suggested the need for an objective experimental branch of the natural sciences that could predict and control behaviour. The emphasis had to be on the practical problems of living. The Second World War brought additional support for the need for readily available, effective psychotherapy that was affordable. The Veterans Administration in the United States became a major source for the support and development of psychotherapeutic interventions and techniques. But it was not until the work of B.F. Skinner during the 1950s, that the development of the modern behavioural schools of psychotherapy gained popularity. Behaviourism placed its emphasis and goals on observable behaviours and direct experimental evidence, with interventions and techniques based largely on modern learning theory.

What we call the Third Wave is humanistic psychology, as exemplified in the work of Abraham Maslow and his theory of self-actualization, which gained prominence, like behavioural therapy, in the 1950s. At the same time, Carl Rogers's development of client-centred psychotherapy ushered in this new wave of humanism. The goal of psychotherapy was the full awareness and expression of feelings for the sole purpose of personal growth. The humanistic school was a reaction and response to what was seen as the mechanical, impersonal, formal, hierarchical mode of the psychoanalytic school and what was seen as the scientific, cold, distanced approach of the behaviourists. The humanistic school of psychotherapy endorsed interventions and techniques for experiencing, emphasizing and expressing choice, values, self-realization and the potential for uniqueness. The humanistic approach was one of phenomenological discovery, emphasizing potential for actualizing and growth, self-determination and person centredness. One of these schools that differs slightly in the use of a large repertoire of interventions and techniques is that of Gestalt therapy, founded by Frederick (Fritz) Perls.

The cognitive school of psychotherapy grew out of both the behaviourist and (rather more subtly) out of the psychoanalytic school (although Ryle's Cognitive-Analytic Therapy has the more obvious link to psychoanalysis). As an extension of Jean Piaget's theories of cognitive development, beginning in the 1950s and 1960s, cognitive psychotherapy shifted the emphasis from looking at the past, on to insight into current cognitive content as the creator of problems and symptoms. Modern cognitive therapy emerged in the mid-1950s with Albert Ellis's Rational Emotive Therapy. Cognitive-behavioural therapies developed in the 1970s.

Another important school, systems theory, is not completely new. Sigmund Freud's coaching of the father in the case of Little Hans (Freud 1909/1955), Alfred Adler's investment in the Child Guidance Movements (1966) were precursors of Nathan Ackerman's (1961) founding of the family therapy movement in the 1930s. During the 1960s, the focus changed from concentration on the individual to the context in which the individual lived and interacted. It was this that gave rise to the systems approach to psychotherapy. Its goal was to change the system, the family or the community, and not just the individual.

Lazarus (1967) introduced eclecticism in the mid-1960s when he developed multi-modal therapy, emphasizing treatment specificity, using different psychotherapeutic interventions and techniques to influence behaviour, affect, sensation, imagery, cognitions, interpersonal relationships and biology.

One of the more recent waves of psychotherapy centres on a strategic plan of change specific to what the client is asking for. The emphasis is to find, develop and apply psychotherapeutic interventions and techniques in the fastest and briefest means possible. Many other schools of psychotherapy such as Neuro-Linguistic Programming, 12-step self-help anonymous, transpersonal, body orients, meridian or energy, hypnosis and psychopharmacology all have their own interventions and techniques, and illustrate the growing evolution of psychotherapy.

Structure of this book

The opening section of each chapter presents the information necessary to understand the school of psychotherapy. The reader is introduced to the core techniques and the people who developed them. Where applicable several different contributors to each wave of psychotherapy are discussed so the reader can see their similarities and their differences. Each school of psychotherapy has its own unique belief about how a problem or symptom is formed (see the companion volume, *Models of Psychopathology*), and therefore tends to have a theoretical perspective on how they are to be resolved. Understanding the basis for resolution is important in understanding the overall process and goal of psychotherapy.

Each chapter lists and describes various psychotherapeutic techniques and interventions specific to that school of psychotherapy. After this description a brief clinical illustration demonstrating the type of intervention or technique in action is often included. At the end of each chapter, there is a brief summary and conclusions as to the core techniques and intervention presented.

Interventions and techniques from a treatment perspective

Psychotherapy is a process whereby an individual who desires change of a symptom or a life problem, or who is seeking personal growth, enters a contractual relationship with a helping professional. It is important to remember that application of the techniques and interventions described in this volume is always aimed at helping to alleviate human suffering.

The goal of psychotherapy is change. There is an old saying that if you always do what you always have done, you will always get exactly what you have always got. Some say that problems come when we keep trying the same thing, yet expecting different results. There are three main areas of change: what a person thinks, what a person feels and the way a person behaves. These areas of change are illustrated throughout the chapters, and later contrasted.

Change in what a person thinks: Changing the way one thinks is the main focus of psychotherapy for both the psychoanalytic and cognitive schools of thought. The psychoanalytic school wishes the patient to gain some insight into her or his current problem, and through finding its roots in developmental patterns that may have become fixed. The cognitive school wishes to challenge the patient to review the way he or she thinks about a situation. While thinking can involve visual representations, these schools of psychotherapy tend to emphasize the language or the talking a person does in their head. This is one of the primary reasons such psychotherapy, or even psychotherapy generally, is often referred to as the 'talking-cure'.

Change in the way a person feels: Changing the way one feels is the focus of psychotherapy for the humanistic school of thought. The humanistic therapist wants the client to find unexpressed feelings (including bodily feelings as well as emotions) and to express them.

Change in the way a person behaves: Changing the way one behaves is the focus of the psychotherapy of the behaviourist school. The behaviourists believe we have learned ineffective or inefficient behaviours that are creating the problem. The therapist wants the patient to learn new, more effective and efficient behaviour patterns to counter clearly specified problems.

Stages of a psychotherapy session

Although our concern in this book is to describe differences between the different therapeutic approaches, it might be possible to attempt to approach psychotherapy generically by outlining six common aspects to the use of interventions in a typical therapy session. Competency in the psychotherapeutic process might then be reflected in the way all six tend to occur in each session (albeit in an order which may differ from that given below, but still forming part of the whole). These aspects are demonstrated again in the sequence of the interventions and techniques in the individual chapters focusing on specific schools of psychotherapeutic thought. They will also be used to contrast and critique the different interventions and techniques in the concluding chapter.

The first aspect is the establishment or re-establishment of rapport. Rapport represents a positive, warm and close relationship between two or more people in the therapeutic relationship, necessary for the therapeutic alliance. The establishment of rapport can be difficult, particularly where the client is anxious, suspicious or hostile. Yet making contact is the first requirement of the therapist in each session. For some therapists, and with many patients, this may be as simple as an everyday greeting at the start of the session, or a gentle inquiry as to how the day or the week has been. Others prefer to wait for the client to open the session, yet try to respond, then, in such a way as to create the right ambience for the work of the session to follow. Without some form of rapport it is difficult to employ any of the other interventions or techniques that a particular school favours.

The second aspect is to gather appropriate and necessary information and to formulate a diagnosis. Some schools are, of course, antipathetic to the idea of any form of diagnosis, smacking as it does of medical labelling. Yet gathering information about the presenting issues or symptoms, or the principal feelings in the session helps to focus the psychotherapist on other interventions and techniques that might be employed. The presenting problem or the dominant feeling may be only the starting point, yet certain interventions may be used to identify these. This is where the client starts from, and may wish to move on from. In some therapies the formulation of treatment goals depends on an accurate assessment of the patient, and later techniques, which will serve this purpose, can then be utilized. Other therapists will use certain interventions to gather a complete mental status evaluation and a diagnosis in order to check that the patient is suited to the treatment that is being offered. Mental status examinations (Wise and Rundel 1988) take into account the current mental capabilities of the client to ensure appropriateness of treatment and facilitate a maximum prognosis of success. Along with the mental status, it may be important to assess the use of any illegal or controlled substances or drugs to assess danger to self and others. Diagnosis takes into account the specific symptoms of the clinical disorder, any personality disorders or developmental problems, the general medical condition that could account for the symptoms or problems, a check of psychosocial and environmental problems and a global assessment of functioning (American Psychiatric Association 1994). But even those therapies that eschew such formal tests or the making of a diagnosis will also use exploratory techniques to enable a fuller picture of the client to be gleaned, greater than that which the client initially presents.

A third aspect is to observe, test and evaluate both the information gathered in the course of the session, as well as the value of the therapist's interventions. Close monitoring of client and of the therapeutic relationship will help to develop deeper rapport and empathy, or in those therapies that have a more formal approach to treatment, more specific calibration of the problems or symptoms which the patient has identified or revealed.

A fourth aspect is the application of certain interventions and techniques specifically to produce change, whether change is seen in terms of certain problems that the patient wishes to resolve, or in terms of insight, behavioural change, personal growth and development or self-actualization.

A fifth aspect is to observe and evaluate which interventions and techniques have proved particularly useful or successful. Since psychotherapeutic interventions are intended to further the interests of the patient or client, it is vital to check out the interventions or techniques that have proved most effective, sometimes as a deliberate technique, sometimes by closer monitoring of a client's response, or in subsequent sessions through evidence of changes in thought, feeling or behaviour.

The sixth aspect involves closing sessions, terminating contracts, rounding off a piece of work, whether it be deep exploration of feelings of the client, or the teaching of some new skills or techniques to the patient. While this will take place in the session, with the patient, it may also include for the therapist some debriefing after the session through supervision and/or consultation. Competent psychotherapists know when and how to use supervision. Debriefing is a means of preventing the therapist's personal issues from clouding the work, as well as checking (as in the fifth aspect above) which interventions have proved valuable, or may be useful in future sessions. The ending of treatment itself, in some orientations, also involves the follow-up of the client to measure long-term results and the effectiveness of the techniques which a particular therapist or therapy has used.

Interventions and techniques from an ethical perspective

Many elements facilitate the ethical application of psychotherapeutic interventions and techniques, but the interventions and techniques of psychotherapy can be abused. To prevent this abuse, ethical guidelines are designed to protect the patient's or client's welfare. Ethical violations of principles (Engler and Goleman 1992) include:

- making suggestions that are immoral, illegal, or harmful;
- interventions that discriminate on grounds of race, religion, gender, age, sexuality, disability, etc.;
- offering services outside the therapist's area of competence;
- offering services when the therapist is in some way incapacitated;
- imposing values;
- avoiding or denying responsibility;
- violating moral or legal standards of the community;
- entering into a dual relationship with the patient or client.

Violations of ethical procedures include:

- not maintaining or protecting confidentiality;
- not obtaining informed consent, not allowing voluntary parti-
  cipation;
- not making appropriate use of resources and referrals;
- offering psychotherapy when the patient or client is already
  engaged in treatment elsewhere;
- and not acting when learning of another professional's unethical
  behaviour.

While in this book the concentration is on what the different
schools claim to be the most therapeutically beneficial techniques
and interventions, the way in which any technique or intervention
can be used to manipulate clients and so dishonour the profession is
not forgotten. In particular it is stressed that within this relatively
brief work only the way in which different therapists work can be
sketched. It is understood that in the majority of schools a long
training, and often continuing supervision, hones these skills into
effective ways of helping the patient; what is described here cannot
be picked up, like a tool from a bench, without thorough knowledge
of its best use and potential dangers.

CHAPTER 2

Psychodynamic and psychoanalytic psychotherapy

The interventions and techniques of the psychodynamic school of psychotherapy have evolved over the 1900s from those first designed to analyse and overcome conflicts that initially Freud understood through the pleasure/reality principle: symptoms were expressions of repressed pain (trauma), which also might have pleasurable (sexual) implications. Analysis sought to uncover these repressions and replace them with adaptation to the reality principle; the suggestion was that some trauma were in fact fantasy rather than actual.

The course of the development and modification of the techniques originally used by Freud is both long and intricate. Pulver (1995) provides a comprehensive modern view of the techniques of 'the frame', the real versus the therapeutic alliance versus transference, 'free association', 'free floating attention', abstinence and other techniques, some of which are covered below (Freud 1912/1955).

Paolino (1981) sees the classical psychoanalytic interventions and techniques as designed to achieve several goals. The first was to expose the client to unresolved, unconscious, intra-psychic conflicts from their past that were causing symptoms in the present. Next, interventions and techniques were to achieve a regressive transference and to utilize the psychotherapeutic relationship to resolve the conflict. This would alter the psychic structure based on this new conscious awareness and insight. Analytic methods were aimed at discovering and analysing repressed feelings, emotions, or conflicts principally through such techniques as free association and dream analysis. But the development of technique has come a substantial way from the older conflict model. The contributions of the Object Relations theorists and specifically the Self Psychological school has brought psychodynamic techniques into closer alignment with those findings on the process of therapy which emphasize the relationship between the client and the therapist (Stolorow *et al.* 1987; Rowe and MacIsaac 1995; St Clair 2000).

The interventions and techniques of the psychoanalytic school of psychotherapy, including the emphasis on the neutrality of the analyst, were designed to facilitate communication; to promote transference as an aid to identification of early relationships in the client's history; to identify defence mechanisms, such as compensation, denial, displacement, dissociation, identification, intellectualization, projection, rationalization, reaction formation, regression, repression, sublimation, and withdrawal; and to find the unconscious conflicts they are protecting. Modern developments have largely diminished the conflict model and the emphasis on neutrality. Analysts such as Winnicott and Kohut have emphasized the development of the relationship with a view to assisting the client to re-commence development. Though these and other theorists have varying allegiances to the techniques of classical psychoanalysis they nevertheless emphasize the role of relating rather than conflict as the basis of therapy and hence the centrality of the relationship in the design and conduct of techniques. More recently, the major focus has been on the elucidation of the therapeutic relationship and the poles of delayed development (Kohut 1984).

Carl Gustaf Jung (1875–1961) after working closely with Freud introduced new concepts to analytical theory and practice. Jung's approach to psychotherapy, it might be argued, was a more obviously co-operative one than that of Freudian analysis, although arguments about activity and passivity are not clear-cut. The sofa, preferred in Freudian analysis, appears to encourage passivity, and appears to make the patient inferior in being supine while the analyst imperiously sits upright behind the patient's head. Jung's preference for face to face work indicates a more equal relationship. Jung opposed the Freudian couch because of Jung's emphasis on equality and mutuality, and objections have been raised against the couch unless a patient is 'very strung up and tense' (Adler 1966) although, as Samuels (1985, Ch. 6) points out in the chapter devoted to the analytic process other British Jungians such as Fordham argue in favour of the couch. Jung's particular concern for equality (Samuels prefers the term 'mutuality' as more accurate) means that both analyst and patient are involved in projection, introjection and defences, and are involved in a joint dialectical procedure. As Samuels observes, Jung, in criticizing Freud and Alfred Adler for having 'technical rules' and 'pet emotive ideas' (Jung 1982: 17, para. 203) is himself being narrow-minded (Samuels 1985: 174). Freudians might equally argue that the patient is far from inferior, and that, for example, the supine position is to encourage the patient's free flow of associations and ensure greater possibilities of communication.

Jung developed the Word Association test (see Jung 1982) as well as the use of painting and dream interpretation that went beyond the family or individual to the universal archetypes and the collective unconscious. Jung also began the use of assignments between sessions to add to the psychotherapeutic process, including reflection, recording dreams and imagining. One goal of Jungian psychotherapy is to integrate the repressed or unresolved aspects of the personal unconscious and bring the patient into contact with the collective unconscious. To accomplish this, Jungian psychotherapy focuses on the present and future striving.

Core interventions and techniques

The developing goal of Freudian psychoanalysis was to resolve the conflicts between the id, ego and the superego and with the outside world. Freud himself appears to have used a fairly authoritative approach. Although he abandoned, early on, hypnosis, as being too passive a technique, and later what he called the pressure technique of placing his hand on the patient's head while he addressed questions to them, he nevertheless could be quite forceful when he thought he understood what was at issue:

> I determined to precipitate the decisive explanation. I therefore questioned her about the causes and circumstances of the first appearance of the pains. . . . It had inevitably become clear to me long since what this was all about. . . . I put the situation drily before her. . . . She complained . . . [that] I had talked her into it . . . It was a long time before my two pieces of consolation . . . made any impression on her.
>
> (Freud and Breuer 1895: 224–7)

We notice here the determination in Freud and also his comforting of Elizabeth von R. in her distress at his interpretation.

Freud was persuaded by another patient to drop much of his questioning and listen to her (Freud and Breuer 1895: 119–20), and he began to understand the value of what became the fundamental psychoanalytic requirement of free association. He would, it appears, instruct his patients initially as follows:

> What you tell me must differ in one respect from an ordinary conversation . . . You will notice that as you relate things various thoughts will occur to you which you would like to put aside on the grounds of certain criticisms and objections. . . . You must never give in to these criticisms, but must say it in spite of them . . .
>
> (Freud 1913: 134–5)

Free association is used to help uncover unconscious material: thoughts, feelings, dreams and even awareness of bodily sensations. The lack of social, logical or appropriate controls produces a permissive environment and minimizes the ego defence (at least the conscious ego defence), although patients may still hold things back out of shame. The freer a person can be, the more unconscious material has opportunity to find expression. The stream of consciousness produces symbols that might be interpreted as well as recurrent themes. The material produced by the client will demonstrate emerging themes about which the client will be encouraged to generate further associations. Freud considered free association one of the most important psychotherapeutic techniques used in psychoanalysis, although in using it a client might be informed that free associating is a difficult process and that a person cannot continue doing it indefinitely. Alternating with it is the need to reflect, with the analyst, on the material, through the co-operation of the working alliance.

Anna Freud (1966) presents free association as a method of working upon which the patient's defence mechanisms intrude and create resistance. To that end the psychoanalyst's task is to first recognize the defence mechanism and only then to restore the material protected by the defence mechanism, turning the attention from analysis of the ego to the id. In more modern approaches to defence (Wastell 1999) the role of free association is to assist the client to map their world-view (à la Bowlby), to detect avoided areas of their experience and hence to explore aversive motives (Lichtenberg *et al.* 1996).

Parallel with this process in the patient is the free-floating attention of the analyst:

> Just as the patient must relate everything that his self-observation
> can detect . . . so the doctor must put himself in a position to
> make use of everything he is told . . . without substituting a
> censorship of his own . . . he must turn his own unconscious
> into a receptive organ towards the transmitting unconscious of
> the patient.
>
> (Freud 1912: 115)

Although it is obvious that Freud himself was not always neutral or
abstinent in his interventions, the development of technique in
Freudian and Kleinian analysis was to stress neutrality or abstinence,
with the intention of avoiding the interference of the analyst with
the stream of consciousness, projections, transference, etc. The analyst tries to become a blank screen.

The safety of the frame

While analysis, through the couch, through free association, and
the relative passivity of the analyst encourages the free flow of
unconscious material, this takes place within the security of a clear
framework, the analytic 'hour' – usually 50 minutes – and clear rules
about starting and ending on time, the frequency of sessions, as well
as, normally, no contact between sessions. The 'frame' has been
seen as of particular significance by the psychoanalyst and commu-
nicative psychotherapist Robert Langs (1982), who states that a 'se-
cured' frame offers the best conditions for a safety and trust so that
a patient can feel free to communicate openly. The frame 'offers the
opportunity to resolve the patient's symptoms through insight and
understanding, rather than through a mode of cure designed for
action-discharge, immediate relief and pathological gratification and
defense' (Langs 1982: 326). The analytic framework established in
psychoanalysis contains both the patient and the analyst. In the
following example, the therapist explains some of this to the client,
thus inviting the client to understand the process and promoting
one of the features that Greenson emphasizes as being essential to
the working alliance (Greenson 1967: 214): 'All new or strange procedures are explained to the patient. I always explain to the patient
why we ask him to try to associate freely and why we prefer to use
the couch. I wait for the patient's questions or responses before I
suggest that he try the couch.'

Illustration

>T: As part of our work together there are some important guidelines that I want to explain to you before we start today. I hope we will do important work at a level appropriate to your needs. This means that in order to keep you safe I will be making sure that you and I are clear about the roles each of us plays and the expectations of what therapy is about. This will mean that the time we spend will be clearly understood by us and that arrangements for payment and appointment times are agreed on.
>
>C: This sounds a little formal and tight. Why is this important?
>
>T: Well, the frame, as it is often called, for therapy is about containing what goes on to this time together. This means we try to ensure that the work we do here does not interfere with your outside life, for example other relationships with friends and family.
>
>C: What if I need to go over time or have an extra appointment?
>
>T: The guidelines are able to be stretched but only for very good reasons. In one sense, the frame and its application are one of the ways in which I will exercise my care for you as we work together.
>
>　You may wish to start by sitting as you are now, but I also invite you, when it feels OK for you, to use this couch, where you can lie down, facing away from me. This will allow you to tell me what you are thinking without any concerns about my reactions. I will sit and listen to you, for the most part without interruption. Just say whatever comes into your mind. If that feels all right, we can perhaps begin. I'd like you to tell me everything that comes to mind, try not to hold anything back.
>
>C: This feels a bit strange just to talk. Though I have to admit it feels nice just to have someone listen to me without me having to be concerned about what they are thinking. Usually I'm the one who listens and gets told what to do. I remember growing up, my parents lived by the rule that children should be seen and not heard. I'm not so sure they even liked us to be seen either.

Interpretation of resistance and transference

The role of interpretation in a psychodynamically informed therapy is to enable the client to become aware of their psychic structures and how these are directing and impacting on their lives. An analytical attitude interprets the content back to the client, facilitating insight and resolution. Loewenstein (1982: 3–4) provides the following definition: 'In psychoanalysis this term [interpretation] is applied to those explanations, given to patients by the analyst, which add to their knowledge about themselves'. The analyst also pays close attention to unconscious disclosures of the presence of defences (see also the companion volume in this series, *Resistance, Barriers and Defences*).

Psychodynamic interpretation of the resistance is made initially to enlighten the client as to the role of defence mechanisms in preventing information from coming into consciousness. Resistance is functional and dysfunctional at the same time. The interpretation of a resistance is undertaken with caution so as to progress the client's self-understanding. Interpretations may also be made of the transference – the tendency the patient has to project or transfer feelings and properties associated with their parental and other significant figures on to the therapist (see the companion volume in the series, *Transference and Projection*). How the patient feels about the analyst may be an indication of these same affects in relation to significant others. Anna Freud (1966) emphasized the interpretation of libidinal impulses, defence and acting out in the transference.

To offer an interpretation a therapist must have assembled a good amount of information about the client and their relationships. This especially includes their relationship to the therapist. Interpretations are usually tied to the here-and-now material of the therapeutic encounter before they are linked to outside situations. The phrasing of the interpretation needs to reflect a solid grounding in the material that the client has presented, and it may well be that the initial elucidation of particular emotions associated with the situation comes more from inquiry rather than pronouncement. The content of the interpretation is usually heavily dependent on the particular psychoanalytic theory that the therapist uses to guide her or his practice: Freudian, Kleinian, Object Relations being the three principal theories. Modern psychodynamic approaches, especially of Kohut and others emphasizes the striving for relatedness as the overarching concept that guides most interpretations.

Illustration

C: Like I was saying my parents really thought 'children should be seen and not heard'. And even though it's nice that your listening to me, I'm not sure what you are thinking. It feels uncomfortable, you just sitting there and not being involved in a conversation: that gets to me.

T: It's interesting that this theme of my passivity has come up a few times. It seems to me that this has connection to your experience of your parents and the way they treated you. They made you feel ignored. My sitting and listening also seems like you might feel I'm ignoring you. How does that sound to you?

C: I suppose that's possible. They weren't very involved and it has left a sore spot. I mean I am constantly looking for the attention and involvement of others in anything I do.

T: And when you think about that how do you feel about it?

C: I feel a bit angry, if I'm really honest.

T: If you're feeling angry with me at the moment I guess that could be how you also felt as a child.

Dream interpretation

Dream interpretation has been a significant part of psychoanalysis since its inception, much used, of course, by Freud in his own self-analysis. Indeed, the analysis of the transference came later, since at first transference was seen as a form of resistance rather than as an aid to the process. Freud viewed dreams as reflecting the unconscious waking states of individuals. During sleep the mental functions become more primitive, minimizing the control of defences and the ego. The older conflict model of psychoanalysis identified manifest and latent content aspects of dreams. The manifest content can come from everyday chance stimuli and memories. Freed repressed wishes find expression as latent content within the dream. The content is therapeutic in that, finding expression, and through interpretation, the patient can become aware and gain insight into their unconscious processes and conflicts.

There is nevertheless more debate now about the value of dreams in psychotherapy. 'Most analysts would agree that the dream has lost its unequivocal centrality in the analytic endevor', writes Flanders in the introduction to *The Dream Discourse Today* (1993: 21) (see also the companion volume, *Words and Symbols*). From the Object Relations perspective in psychoanalytic psychotherapy, the material of dreams is still very valuable for therapy but not only for repressed material and hence for unresolved conflicts. Dreams may also express unresolved longings with respect to desired relationships. The themes in the dream may be better viewed as the expressions of desired or even feared object relations. Thus when accessing dream material the therapist uses free association to construct the relationship theme.

Illustration

> C: I had a dream last week that was strange. I was walking through a park. I saw a woman in the distance and I thought it was my girlfriend. I ran up to her and when I touched her shoulder, she turned to a stone figure. I woke up – that's all I remember.
>
> T: Can you let your mind wander freely over the dream, maybe starting with any part of it and see where it takes you.
>
> C: You mean like free association?
>
> T: Yes, that's what I mean.
>
> C: Running! And running desperate to catch up with her, wanting to be close but she never seems to respond warmly. Running: I'm thinking of myself like a child running; perhaps running up to my mother for comfort when I'm hurt. Stone – stone cold. That's all I can think of immediately.
>
> T: And perhaps mother not responding, being cold when you wanted help. Seeing me a bit like that too, perhaps, because you want more response from me?

The mutative interpretation

A famous paper within psychoanalytic writing is that of James Strachey (1934) on 'The nature of the therapeutic action of psychoanalysis'. The paper also appears in full in Meissner's (1991) study of the move from interpretation to the relationship in therapy, where he summarizes Strachey's argument, which is further summarized here: 'The analytic objective of bringing the patient's unconscious needs into awareness soon ran afoul of the patient's resistances. . . .

The patient's transference love becomes a motivating force inducing him to give up the resistances and undo the repression' (Meissner 1991: 51).

The transference becomes the central piece of the whole treatment process, and through a series of projections and introjections the patient is able to accept the analyst's interpretations, which then undermine the neurotic process. Interpretations that achieve this aim are called 'mutative'. They have several qualities: 'they must be emotionally immediate . . . specific . . . sufficiently detailed and concrete . . . ought not to be too deep . . . [and] usually take place within the transference' (Meissner 1991: 53).

Meissner traces the developments since Strachey's paper, observing the influence of Object Relations theory, with its new emphasis on the importance of the relationship with others, not just the internal conflicts within the one individual, in the formation of integrated functioning in adult life; of Kohut's self-psychology (see below) and of development theory. The emphasis in the therapeutic process has therefore moved away from a narrow pre-occupation with interpretation, towards seeking an understanding of the conditions in the therapeutic process that are necessary to bring about change.

In the final part of his book, Meissner examines the 'significant ferment in the development of psychoanalytic technique' (Meissner 1991: 151–75). He includes the analyst's inclusion of the ongoing interaction in the immediacy of the here-and-now, less rigid abstinence on the part of the therapist (see below on Lomas and before him Ferenczi), interactive rather than interpretative interventions, emphasis on the holding environment and recognition of the intersubjective process (Atwood and Stolorow 1984: 104). The question of whether these changes make psychoanalysis more effective is beyond the scope of this volume (see the companion volume in the series, *Objectives and Outcomes*). But it is interesting to see the questioning taking place, and the changes in emphasis that have followed, a very good example of which is found in the following sections on Kohut in America and on Lomas in Britain.

Empathic attunement: self-psychology

For Freud, empathy was an essential part of the interpretative process (Freud 1921: 137). Empathy is the ability to put the self in someone else's position ('in their shoes') and appreciate their perspective. This is well examined in other volumes in this series, yet it is important to recognize just how important it is as a part of psychoanalytic therapy as well. The technique of empathic attunement allows the psychotherapist to develop rapport and a relationship based on acceptance. Self-psychology, developed within the psychoanalytic school in America by Heinz Kohut, has stressed just how important the constant use of empathic attunement by the therapist is, in helping to build a cohesive and coherent sense of self in the client. Kohut (1971, 1977, 1984) established self-psychology from his work with narcissistic or self-disorders, that have resulted from a failure in self and object differentiation. Kohut believed that the quality of the therapist–patient interaction created the emotional milieu or therapeutic empathy. His emphasis is on the identification of the affective aspect of the experience. This is the key to understanding the motivation of the client for their current problems and therefore potential points for intervention. The key element in this technique is the articulation of the affect detected by the therapist (see below). Notice that the gender of the therapist has been defined and, from the above example, it may be thought the therapist is a woman (like mother, and the woman in the dream). But transference interpretations do not necessarily have to conform to gender matches with significant others. In the following examples, the therapist is seen more as a father figure.

Illustration

> C: At work I get put down a lot by the boss. I try to meet the demands he puts on me but I never seem to do it right.
> T: The boss seems hard on you?
> C: Yes, that's it; but no harder than on anyone else.
> T: So, it's like being rejected?
> C: Yes it is!
> T: It sounds to me like this rejection is pretty painful.
> C: Yes, painful to the point of not knowing how I can ever be acceptable. Like I want to be in his good books.
> T: He matters more than just as a boss; almost like a friend?
> C: (*Sheepishly*) No. More like a father.

Three types of selfobject transferences

The term selfobject was coined by Kohut to convey the idea that clients (indeed everyone throughout their development) will need from significant others, and especially their therapist, certain specified roles to help them master aspects of their lives and so develop competence. Kohut's ideas have been refined and developed by a number of authors including Basch (1988, 1992, 1995), Lichtenberg (1989) and Lichtenberg, Lachmann and Fosshage (1996).

One of the most helpful authors from the point of view of technique is Basch. His work on the concept of selfobject transference has been seminal in operationalizing what can be confusing to the non-Kohutian trained therapist. The three transferences Basch outlines (1992) are:

1 Kinship: this is the identification with someone at the feeling level. This person detects and articulates by action and words the unspoken feelings of the situation.
2 Idealizing: reliance on the ability to trust and confide in someone who is dependable. This enables the client to draw on the experience of this person.
3 Validation: being understood in a complete manner both feelings and understanding of the situation or need the client is facing.

Basch asserts that these are three aspects of the good therapist in action. The way therapists use this technique is essentially to pay very close attention to their internal and empathic modes of operating and to articulate the developmental needs of the client as expressed in the therapy. Taking the previous illustration and expanding it we can identify the types of transferences most at work in each interaction.

Illustration: Kinship

> *C:* At work I get put down a lot by the boss. I try to meet the demands he puts on me but I never seem to do it right.
> *T:* The boss seems hard on you? (*Kinship: noting the feeling precursor 'hard'.*)
> *C:* Yes, that's it; but no harder than on anyone else.
> *T:* So, it's like being rejected?
> *C:* Yes it is!
> *T:* It sounds to me like this rejection is pretty painful? (*Kinship: noting the feeling 'painful'.*)
> *C:* Yes, painful to the point of not knowing how I can ever be acceptable. Like I want to be in his good books.

T: He matters more than just as a boss; almost like a friend?
C: (*Sheepishly*) No. More like a father.

Illustration: Idealizing

C: (*Sheepishly*) No. More like a father.
T: Someone you might depend on? (*Note the implication of idealizing.*)
C: Yes, I sometimes feel that way here, but better. (*The client idealizes the therapist.*)
T: You mean you can draw on me and our time together to help you cope. (*Therapist makes explicit the value of the idealizing transference.*)

Illustration: Validating

C: Yes; but you listen and seem to understand it from my perspective.
T: So it sounds like you get the picture that I understand you from your viewpoint.
C: Yes, and that I'm on the right track, that's what is important. (*The validation is not just about understanding, but about recognizing and articulating the client's construction of meaning as being valid.*)

The process of feedback within responses to the transference is to enable the client to recommence relational development, with the aim being to achieve a sense of competence and therefore autonomy which is open to others.

Questioning technique

Amongst a number of former analysts, who have felt the need to quit the orthodox psychoanalytic societies, a particular critic is Peter Lomas, whose several books since 1973 have criticized many aspects of psychoanalytic technique (see King 1999 for the most complete assessment of his work). He questions, for example, the centrality of the interpretation and the abstinence of the psychotherapist; that is, revealing little about his or herself, using the self as a blank screen. He is critical of psychoanalytic training on technique and of adhering rigidly to the rules of procedure that have been taught. He believes that on occasion there is good reason for some physical contact; he emphasizes the importance of relating to patients as ordinary human beings. Lomas no doubt criticizes a particular type of analyst and we have to be careful not to imagine that every analyst fits his stereotype, or indeed that every analyst uses identical techniques. Accounts of being in analysis, stories of working with some of the famous names in psychoanalysis, often reveal the true humanity of those practitioners who might be held up as models of classical technique: Freud, Anna Freud and Winnicott are just some of those whose practice was not rigidly 'text-book'.

Stereotypical it may be, yet Lomas (1987: 11) has identified a strong criticism of analytic technique, and not just of particular expressions of technique, but of the concept of technique as a whole: 'Because I hold the view that psychotherapy is not a technique – whether scientific or interpretative – I am at a loss to know how to present it'. Lomas (1985) instead chooses to describe and discuss some of his experiences of being a psychotherapist, still very much understanding the process itself from a psychodynamic perspective, but working with much more flexibility.

Such flexibility extends to self-disclosure, when he feels it may be useful to the patient; and to the use of touch, again when he feels it is appropriate. This makes him very different from most psychoanalytic psychotherapists, at least those who write about what they do, although there is an historical precedent in Ferenczi, who experimented with mutual analysis, which involved the analyst acquainting his patients with his own weaknesses and feelings, permitting physical contact, etc. (see Dupont 1985). Ferenczi lost Freud's friendship through his experimentation, although Ferenczi constantly saw his new techniques as part of ongoing research into practice, 'advanced by new routes' (Dupont 1985: xiv) – the three books of his papers all include 'technique of psychoanalysis' in their title (Ferenczi 1950). (Aspects of the therapist's engagement with the client, which move beyond the learning of technique to drawing on the therapeutic relationship, are examined more closely in the companion volume in this series, *The Therapist's Use of Self*.)

Summary and conclusions

The interventions and techniques described in this chapter are a small subset of the overall process of psychodynamically orientated therapy. Their purpose is more effectively to explore the depth and complexity of a client's life and to provide opportunity for the client to gain a fuller understanding of where they have come from, and the ways in which they presently function. This process takes time and commitment from both the therapist and the client, and while much psychoanalytic therapy is a long-term commitment, the development in recent years of short-term psychodynamic therapy has meant more focus on particular areas, in itself developing a 'technique' for brief work, such as focusing on the ending. Similarly the development of child analysis required other techniques for communication. This was especially true in play therapy (Klein 1932; Freud 1946). Even a spatula and the squiggle (Winnicott 1975) were used. Group therapy developed its own adaptation of techniques (Bion 1959; Foulkes and Anthony 1965; Pines 1985). Nor should the work of other experiments in practice be forgotten, such as R.D. Laing (1965) and others in the community at London's Kingsley Hall (see for example Schatzman 1971).

Modern psychodynamic theory emphasizes the importance of the therapeutic relationship, including the real relationship. This is a significant development from Freud's original concepts of the detached observer. The establishment of a good working alliance is also crucial for the proper implementation of any technique.

Psychoanalytic literature is rich in reflection on theory and practice, although the basic elements of therapeutic technique are less commonly described (see, however, Greenson's (1967) magisterial but uncompleted treatment of the subject). If at times the technique has become the subject of caricature, it is important to recognize that Freud pioneered a method of treatment which distinguished him from the psychiatrists of his day, and that his techniques have been taken up, sometimes in adapted form, sometimes developed further in identifying the listening and responding, by a host of therapeutic approaches that have diverged more considerably on theory than on practice. These shall be examined, showing the similarities and differences, in subsequent chapters.

CHAPTER 3

Behavioural psychotherapy

The modern practice of behaviour therapy started during the 1950s, primarily as a reaction to psychoanalysis. Behaviour therapy uses different techniques that aim directly at changing problem behaviours through altering the conditions that maintain such behaviours. Behavioural psychotherapy is particularly oriented towards action: patients learn and practice new adaptive behaviour in the session, and develop this through homework assignments.

The methods of the behavioural school of psychotherapy are generally all derivatives of the classical learning experiments used with animals. The old Pavlovian experiment of teaching a dog to salivate to a bell by associating it with the stimulus of food became the basis of early behavioural psychotherapy. It was observed that a new conditioned response could be associated with a naturally occurring unconditioned response to a specific stimulus. The conditioned response could then elicit the original unconditioned response. It was later seen that by positive reinforcement a desirable behaviour could be helped to occur more often. Likewise, with negative or no reinforcement less desirable behaviour was less likely to occur, or could diminish until the behaviour became extinct. Behaviour psychotherapy is based on learning theory. The goal of behaviour modification is therefore to extinguish old maladaptive behaviours and replace them or elicit new ones. Behaviour therapy refers to both operant and classical conditioning. A certain amount of operant conditioning occurs in the most non-directive psychotherapies through the psychotherapist's approval (positive reinforcement) or disapproval (negative reinforcement) to the patient's verbal and non-verbal expressions. Under classical conditions, much like associating or transferring salivation to the sound of a bell, a psychotherapist begins to re-associate or transfer a new response to an old stimulus.

The psychotherapist first makes an assessment of the sequence and situations that lead up to the unwanted behaviour. He or she then designs and implements a programme of reinforcement to modify this behaviour. One technique is systematic desensitization, which uses progressive incremental steps of conditioning. Operant conditioning, such as the use of a token economy, modifies behaviour by the application of rewards or tokens for the performance of wanted behaviours. Aversion therapy uses negative consequences such as an electrical shock to modify behaviour.

Positive reinforcement consists of the rewarding of a desired new behaviour with something the client would enjoy. Negative reinforcement is the punishment of an undesirable behaviour through negative consequences. In extreme cases, negative reinforcement becomes aversion therapy where the conditions of continuing an unwanted behaviour are severe enough that the client is conditioned against acting on them. Reinforcement can be scheduled at fixed intervals (or rations) or on a continuous basis. It may also be totally withheld so that an undesirable behaviour receives no reinforcement and, it is hoped, leads to removal of the incentive for that behaviour. Applied in a therapeutic community, reinforcement becomes a token economy in which an individual receives a token as positive reinforcement, which can be redeemed later for some tangible reward.

Joseph R. Cautela and Albert J. Kearney in *Covert Conditioning* (Zeig 1992) state that a subject can be influenced on three levels. The first is their overt behaviour, such as walking and talking. The second is their covert physiological behaviour, such as internal organ activity like heart rate, galvanic skin response, etc. The third is their covert psychological behaviour, such as thoughts and feelings. The goals of behavioural psychotherapeutic interventions and techniques are first to increase the self-control, competence, independence, self-confidence and skills a client has over a problem; and second to increase the level of reinforcement for these new behaviours in their life.

Behavioural assessment and interviewing (Granvold 1994) stress the gathering of information so that all interventions and techniques can be goal directed. It is necessary to get a brief description of the problem, the development of the problem in relationship to its precipitants, its timing of occurrence and predisposing factors. In the description of the problem behaviour, all factors must be taken into account, such as the behaviour, cognitive, affective and physiological characteristics. Questions are addressed about what, when, where, how often, with whom, how distressing and how disruptive is the problem behaviour. Information on the contextual variables and the maintaining factors is also considered. Other information used to decide the appropriate therapeutic approach includes methods of avoidance of the problem, coping resources and assets, psychiatric and medical history, previous treatment and responsiveness, the individual's beliefs about the problem, mood and mental states, and their psycho-social situation.

Core interventions and techniques

From the behaviourist's point of view, it is maladaptive behaviours only that create problems. These behaviours have been learned and conditioned through past experiences. Since the behaviours are the problem, resolution is focused directly on both stopping the maladaptive behaviour and demonstrating a behaviour that works more satisfactorily within the desired context.

Assessment

Behavioural assessment (Mischel 1968) was developed to assess what a client does rather than what characteristics a client has. It provides a highly specific picture of the presenting problem behaviour and the immediate determinants and consequences. This process is used to map with great detail the behavioural sequences, especially triggers and environmental cues. The following illustration is taken from Wilson, Spence and Kavanagh (1989: 54–68). The client has presented with depression, and the therapist asks a series of questions, such as:

- In general, how have you been feeling in the last week?
- When do you feel best during the day?
- When do you feel worst during the day?
- How much change in your mood do you feel during the day?
- What work do you do?
- Do you enjoy it?
- Are you able to accomplish the usual amount of work at the moment?
- Do you go out with people after work? (If yes) What sort of things do you do?
- Do you enjoy this time?

The therapist's aim is to gather as much relevant information as possible, so that the context of the problem can be well mapped and techniques then used to assist this client within the context of a detailed understanding of his or her circumstances.

Relaxation training

Relaxation training can be used to counter fear, anxiety and tension, and may be a useful precursor to other aspects of the therapy. (Its focus is to learn to relax the skeletal muscles.) The most popular, progressive or systematic relaxation, teaches a client to tense and then relax muscles throughout the body. The training helps a client distinguish between a tensed and relaxed state. They may then begin to relax in any context that previously would have caused tension. There are a number of methods for training in relaxation: one of the most widely used is that based on Bernstein and Borkovic (1973). The following description is derived from Barlow and Rapee (1997: 22–7) for stress management using deep muscle relaxation. Ideally, this procedure should be audio taperecorded so that the client can practise it twice a day throughout the period between sessions. This takes several sessions to perfect and this only if the client is able to practise it in between sessions. The therapist is well advised to regard this step as crucial to a range of other behavioural techniques and worth considerable investment of therapeutic time (see Brown *et al.* 1993: 156–7 for guidance on the extensive work needed to be done in mastering the skill of progressive muscular relaxation).

Illustration

> *T:* I would like to introduce you to a relaxation technique which will be useful in a number of ways . . .
>
> Settle yourself into the chair and sit in a comfortable position but not with arms or legs crossed, just sitting upright, be as loose as you can . . .
>
> Now start to pay attention to your breathing. In and out slowly and deeply.
>
> Take a deep breath and hold it (held for 10 seconds) . . . Now release the breath . . .

I want you to make a fist with both your hands by
starting with the palms pointing down. Bend the fist
upward toward the lower arm . . .
Now relax your arms, just let them settle . . .

The therapist takes the patient through other limbs and areas of
the body, the toes, thighs, abdomen, shoulders, neck, facial muscles,
forehead, etc.

Systematic desensitization

Systematic desensitization allows a client to confront a fearful
situation or stimulus gradually. Wolpe (1958, 1981, 1982) initially
developed this approach for the treatment of fear and anxiety.
The procedure involves three steps. The first is learning a different
response to anxiety such as deep relaxation or assertive behaviour.
In the second step, the client establishes an anxiety hierarchy of
small specific gradual situations or stimuli leading towards greater
intensity (see Kaplan *et al.* 1994: 853–4 for some very detailed hier-
archies). The third step is for the client to practise the incompatible
response within each gradual step until they reach the ability to
stay relaxed or assertive within the originally anxiety provoking
situation. The key to the effectiveness of this technique is the
construction of the steps in the anxiety hierarchy. These must be
fine grained enough to enable the client to move through the steps
without experiencing an unbearable increase in anxiety. Systematic
desensitization should not be used where the anxiety is not specific,
or is free floating.

Illustration

This illustration addresses a client who has a fear of, or is anxious
about, public speaking:

    T: You mentioned that you had a fear of speaking in public,
        is that right?
    C: Yes, I really get upset and very agitated.
    T: I would like to understand more fully your experience of
        this fear so I would like to explore it in some detail, if that
        is alright?

C: Yes, I'd really like to get over it.

T: Let's start by you telling me the situations in which you have this fear.

C: It happens when I have to speak at work, to give a report or address my section about changes to work practices.

T: And at other times?

C: I suppose I also get a feeling of it when I'm at parties and I end up telling a funny story. It also happened when I had a new worker start the other week and I had to tell her about the job. Isn't that odd?

T: These seem to be quite a range of situations. What I would like you to do now is to put them in order from the least fearful to the most fearful. Just do it without too much thought.

C: I think the worst is the public speaking especially reporting on the section's production.

T: OK. What is the next worst? (*Going with the client's order may be more useful but this is an individual therapist's decision.*)

T: We now have your anxiety hierarchy around the situation of public speaking. There are 15 items . . .

The next step is to use the relaxation techniques, which have been previously learned. In the next session therefore the therapist asks the patient to relax and imagine the least difficult of the anxiety producing situations in the public speaking hierarchy.

T: Imagine the scene in full: Where is it? Who is there? (*And so on*) Signal when you have the scene clearly in your mind by raising your index finger.

This procedure is repeated over a number of sessions gradually going through the hierarchy. The therapist moves onto the next item in the hierarchy only when the client reports much reduced levels of anxiety in the session. The next step in the process is gradual exposure to the real situation perhaps (and where practicable) with the therapist accompanying the patient.

Exposure and flooding

Exposure or flooding (Spiegler and Guevremont 1998) is another behavioural therapy technique used for reducing fear and anxiety.

The client is exposed to the actual feared situation and must stay in that situation until the fear reaches a peak and declines. Ideally, the patient is not permitted to opt out of the situation. He or she may be encouraged to imagine the feared situation if actual exposure is unrealistic or unsafe. The therapist may also introduce a gradual exposure by introducing larger amounts of exposure over many trial experiences. This technique is thus the opposite of systematic desensitization. There is no use of relaxation. Patients with heart problems and or similar conditions that would be made worse by such levels of anxiety are not good candidates for this procedure.

Illustration

The patient, Chris, has a fear of heights. The therapist first invites him to engage with this fear by staying in the therapist's office and imagining that he is on a high building. The therapist assures him he is there, talking him through it. Chris agrees to the procedure and, having closed his eyes, is taken by the therapist through an imaginary scene, entering the tallest building in the city, walking into the foyer, getting into the lift and going to the top floor of the building. This exercise is taken slowly, with plenty of time for the patient to maintain the relaxation that the therapist has taught him.

The therapist takes Chris in his imagination out of the lift, on to the observation deck, monitoring Chris's reactions, asking Chris to describe how it feels, encouraging him to stay with the imagined scene for as long as he can. The therapist's support is very important, since exposure only works if the patient is able to go through the experience and survive it, thereby achieving a sense of mastery. Otherwise the exercise may become just another instance of failure.

Assertiveness training

This technique is used to assist people in acting more positively and confidently in specific situations. A distinction is made between *aggression* that can be destructive and *assertion* that is usually more constructive in relating to others. Specific language and behaviours are taught relating to the situation or context in which new assertion skills are needed or requested. Patients are taught a different model of desired behaviour. They can rehearse these behaviours and expressions in a safe context, sometimes in a group, before trying them in the real life situation.

Modelling (Bandura 1969) is another tool, where the model is a person who is regarded as a standard of excellence to imitate. A patient is encouraged to act as if they had the same desired behaviour as another, and adaptive behaviours are demonstrated for the patient to copy. The use of modelling in behavioural interventions is widespread and the therapist may become the model, as long as the patient has a realistic view of the therapist; but not if the patient perceives too much of a gap between themselves and the therapist.

It will be illustrated here within the context of assertiveness training. The 'therapist as model' is the process being shown. It is assumed that the client in this illustration does have a good relationship with his therapist.

Illustration

In this example it is shown how assertiveness and modelling are combined in the situation of a client who gets pushed around. The therapist enacts the behaviour not just describes it. This is central to the concept of modelling.

> *T:* We were talking about different situations where you feel you are pushed around.
> *C:* Yes, I don't get much respect from my work colleagues or even people at the corner shop.
> *T:* At the corner shop? Tell me a bit more about that.
> *C:* When I'm buying some groceries I stand in line but other people just push in and get served first.
> *T:* OK. Let's think about the sorts of behaviours that go on. Tell me a bit about what you do at the counter.
> *C:* I stand there politely.
> *T:* Politely? Can you stand up and show me what that means.
> *C:* (*Stands, slightly bent forward in a somewhat submissive pose.*)
> *T:* Now ask for some groceries the way you normally do.
> *C:* 'Could I have a small carton of milk and a half a dozen eggs, please.' (*C's voice is soft and undemanding.*)
> *T:* Here's how it looks to me. (*The therapist replicates the pose, including asking for goods in a soft voice.*)
> *C:* That's about right.
> *T:* Let's see if we can do it differently. (*The therapist stands more upright, looks straight ahead and asks for the groceries in*

a clear, authoritative voice, which is neither loud nor aggressive.) How was that Bill?

C: It sounds more like you mean business.

T: How about you try it?

C: (*Now stands in the same pose as the therapist, and repeats the previous request, a little strained, but more assertive.*)

T: How did that feel?

C: I felt stronger. I like it.

Behavioural rehearsal or role-playing

Role-playing, like modelling, encourages patients temporarily to act as if they are someone else, perhaps someone who already possesses the skill or ability they would like to demonstrate in their own interactions. They play the role of the other person and respond as they would. This technique is often used to assess and teach social skills.

Illustration

T: Chris, you say you want to be able to talk to a woman at work whom you like?

C: Yes, but I get tongue tied and go all red when I try.

T: What about we start by trying to role-play what it would be like talking with her.

C: OK.

T: You can role-play either yourself or the woman.

C: I'll try being Joan – that's her name.

T: And I'm you. (*The therapist is again taking on a modelling stance.*)

T: Hi Joan, how are you today?

C: I'm well, thank you; and how are you?

T: Fine. What did you do over the weekend?

C: I went water-skiing.

T: That's good – I think it's a great sport.

C: Yes, I went with my brother and his family.

T: What got you interested in water-skiing?

C: My parents did it, and so I've been doing it since I was a child.

T: You must be quite good at it by now.

C: Can we stop and talk about this? I wouldn't be able to tell her how good she was.

T: I think you need to be able to show interest in someone else's activities. That's why I focused on her.

C: I keep thinking that I'm not good at much and so she won't think much of me when she finds that out. (*Notice here how Chris's cognitive processes have been brought out by the role-playing.*)

T: Role-playing is a way of practising an actual conversation, though your thoughts are also important. For the moment let's focus on the actions and then look at how you're feeling. I'm going to reverse roles now. I want you to be yourself while I play Joan. (*The role-play is conducted from at least two viewpoints so that the patient can experience the situation as he or she imagines it, from both perspectives.*)

Self-management or control programmes

These programmes (Ferster *et al.* 1962; Goldiamond 1965) set the stage for later cognitive interventions and techniques by discussing the internal processes as subject to behavioural control. Self-control includes monitoring, assessment, evaluation and reinforcement.

Self-monitoring (Hawton *et al.* 1989) is a technique of gathering information about many factors effecting the problem behaviour. Patients keep charts, logs or journals. They record very specific information. Usually, as a minimum, they log the date, the time, the affective state or mood, the behavioural activities and cognitive thoughts before the behaviour. It is also useful to log the context or situational and interpersonal cues. Other information may include the factors maintaining the behaviour, such as what it helps to avoid, and any immediate consequences or long-term consequences. Patients may then add thoughts on any coping resources that may have prevented the problem behaviours had they been available. Self-monitoring should have specifically and clearly defined targets, for ease and simplicity of recording. The information can be recorded as frequency, duration or other self-rating scales.

Illustration

The therapist is helping the patient with timekeeping, for example, getting to work on time.

 T: Self-management programmes are used to change situations
    and behaviours. It seems to me that your problem with
    getting to work on time is one for which it may be very
    useful.
 C: How does it work?
 T: Let's start by defining the situation as you want it to
    be.
 C: I want to get to work on time or even ahead of time.
 T: Let's start with getting to work on time. (*The therapist
    begins with the more obvious task, ahead of time is a later
    task.*) Throughout this coming week, you will need to
    keep a diary each morning of the things that happen and
    at what time they happen. Be as specific as you can. Make
    sure you carefully record the events that precede specific
    events and that thing that you do. For example what time
    do you get up, how long does it take to breakfast and get
    ready? The sheet I have designed outlines the sort of
    things that you will need to record.

At the next session, when the patient produces the diary, the
therapist helps the patient identify where the problem starts, for
example, not allowing enough time to get ready. The patient is
encouraged to conceptualize the problem, as part of the self-
management process.

 C: I think that I don't allow enough time to get ready in the
    morning.
 T: What do you think will fix this?
 C: Getting up earlier.
 T: Sounds about right. And what will help you achieve this?
    (*Here is an example of using positive reinforcement.*)
 C: I was thinking that if I get to work on time for one week
    I'll go to a show I have been wanting to see for some time.
    (*The reward schedule is designed by the client and if possible it
    is 'segmented' so that the rewards are not too much, but are
    incremental and achievable.*)
 T: Let's write that up in the diary and see how it goes. (*It is
    important that the therapist monitors the programme in order to
    encourage its fulfilment and, if necessary, adjust it to become
    more manageable. Patients often overreach themselves either in
    the goals they set or the reinforcements they design as a
    reward.*)

Diversion

This technique is used as a form of distraction, by deliberately focusing on something else other than the fearful stimulus. In the example above, where Chris is anxious talking to Joan, the therapist might therefore help Chris to imagine what it would be like to be well thought of, or to be in conversation with someone where it is really enjoyable. The therapist may then have Chris role-play this other situation to develop a more positive frame of mind that will ultimately be brought back to the presenting problem situation of talking to Joan.

A variation of this is 'time out', a simple technique of interrupting an unwanted behaviour by requiring the patient to sit quietly. This interruption stops any negative reinforcement that may be occurring, which might therefore perpetuate the unwanted behaviour.

Biofeedback training

Biofeedback should be categorized under behavioural approaches, even though its focus is more on controlling physiological states such as tension, galvanic skin response (sweat), heart rate and brain waves. It is founded on the same conditioned learning theories. Biofeedback uses machines that monitor information for the patient regarding the patient's physiological state, through lights, sounds or metres; for example, their heart rate. By focusing their attention on this feedback, it is possible for a patient to gain more control over their physiological responses, such as lowering heart rate, and thereby also lowering anxiety reactions. (For a further description of this technique, see Thompson 1996: 172.)

Conclusion

The behavioural tradition in psychotherapy has, to a large extent, been subsumed more recently under the cognitive-behavioural approach, which is described in Chapter 5, and in doing so has become closer to some other forms of therapy where thought is understood to be as important as behaviour. The lack of exploration of the meaning of reactions, will be noticeable in the illustrations in this chapter. What fear of heights might stand for is not therefore part of the behaviourist's concern: enabling the fear to be less inhibiting is. Why a patient could not compliment someone on their water-skiing is not relevant. Teaching them that it is good to show an interest in others is relevant. Furthermore, it should be remembered that behaviour therapy has been one of the most effective treatment approaches for a number of disorders, such as phobias; and has proved to be more appealing to patients who are either not interested or motivated by insight or other self-reflective techniques.

A particular strength in this approach is the use of clear assessment of antecedents and monitoring of outcomes (see also the volume in this series, *Objectives and Outcomes*). The relative ease with which it is possible to use quantitative methods of research has added to the reputation of behaviour therapy in those quarters where demonstrable cost-effectiveness is an issue. Aside from this, it is possible to see how there can be occasions in other therapeutic approaches, that are less action-directed, where management and support of specific situations might well draw on some of the techniques described here, and on those that follow in looking at the significance of the cognitive.

The emphasis on assessment in behavioural psychotherapy and the specification of both antecedents and outcomes are contributions that all forms of therapy could benefit from. The behavioural schools have identified and developed the insight that all therapists need to pay very close attention to the client's experience of their situation at the behavioural level and go beyond the conceptual and conjectural of any theory to quantifiable observation.

CHAPTER 4

Humanistic-existential psychotherapy

The interventions and techniques of humanistic psychotherapy were developed out of a response and reaction to the psychodynamic and the behavioural models of psychotherapy. These previous schools seemed both to be deterministic and to lack recognition of the individuality or uniqueness of the person. While psychodynamic interventions and technique tend to aim at cognitive insight, and the behavioural interventions aim at behaviour change, what has become known as the 'third force' of the humanistic school aims at the awareness and expression of affect or feelings.

The humanistic school of psychotherapy views all human beings as having a tendency for natural growth and evolution in a positive direction. It is the blocking or lack of awareness of this process that creates problems. The interventions and techniques of the humanistic-existential schools of psychotherapy also share several characteristics of the psychotherapeutic process. The first is a phenomenological approach that views clients as the experts of their own process of self-discovery. The second is the wish to provide the right milieu to foster the tendency towards positive self-actualization, growth and choice. The third is the facilitation of new meaning to experiences. The fourth characteristic is that the psychotherapeutic process is person centred and process oriented. The humanistic-existential modality of psychotherapy makes contact with the individual patient's or client's process of being and becoming in the world, and facilitates the awareness and expression of feelings.

Three of the major contributors to the interventions and techniques of humanistic psychotherapy are Abraham Maslow, Carl Rogers and Fritz Perls.

Abraham Maslow (1968, 1970) acknowledges the concept of 'self-actualization' as the goal of psychological health. The 'fully human-ness' of the individual is seen as altruistic, dedicated, self-transcending and social. Humanistic psychology for Maslow is a psychology of health, motivated towards peak experiences and creativity. One of Maslow's greatest contributions to humanistic psychology and psychotherapy is his description of an hierarchy of needs. It demonstrates the progressive growth and evolution of the individual human being. He describes our needs as beginning with physical needs, followed by safety and security, followed by love and belonging, followed by esteem and self-esteem, and finally the need for self-actualization.

Carl Rogers (1951, 1961, 1977, 1980) concludes that three conditions are necessary to facilitate the successful use of any psychotherapeutic intervention or technique towards actualization. Rogers believes in the conditions of empathy with the client, congruence or genuineness in the psychotherapist and positive regard. Rogers advocates and emphasizes accepting, recognizing and clarifying feelings. His is a 'steady trend away from technique' (Rogers 1961: 432). Any techniques that are used are therefore only to stress specifically the implementation of particular attitudes. (See also the companion volume in this series, *The Therapeutic Environment*.)

The gestalt school of psychotherapy as developed by Fritz Perls (1947, 1969, 1973, 1975; Perls *et al.* 1951) offers three additional concepts. A psychotherapist must take into account the client's contact with the world outside themselves, their awareness of the specific experience and their willingness to experiment with new ways of being. While most humanistic psychotherapists cloak their interventions and techniques in the simple humanity of the therapeutic relationship, the gestalt approach is very technique oriented. Gestalt means the configuration of the whole in which all parts relate to each other. Symptoms represent alienated, split-off, or disowned parts of the whole self. The goal of psychotherapy is therefore the re-owning and integration of these parts back into the gestalt of the individual.

The humanistic schools of psychotherapy place a larger emphasis in their interventions and techniques (even if they largely dislike such a term), on the process (how) over the content (what and why) and on experience over meaning. The gestalt school (Polster and Polster 1973) takes as its foundation the power of the present moment. It is the experience in the present that counts. The therapist is a uniquely individual instrument. The therapeutic situation particularly facilitates awareness and expression of fulfilment, accentuation, the working-through process and the recovery of old experiences (Polster and Polster 1973). Therapy is too rich and valuable to be strictly limited to the sick.

Due to its greater reliance on techniques to make contact, uncover process and facilitate awareness, the gestalt school of psychotherapy is therefore slightly over-represented in the following sections.

Existential psychotherapy

Existentialism stems from the philosophy of Kierkegaard, Nietzsche and Sartre. As an attempt to grasp reality it accepts that humans are always in a state of being and becoming, which implies always being in a potential state of crisis, anxiety or despair. The emphasis on 'being' is a particularly existential contribution to psychotherapy. Existential psychotherapeutic interventions and techniques help foster a sense of free responsibility and spontaneous creativity as unique and fundamental characteristics of human existence. The interventions and techniques are designed to acknowledge a person's existence in the world, and the limits and responsibilities that entails, while assisting the individual away from the limits of determinism. These interventions and techniques, like the humanistic, focus on the awareness of the dynamic process of growth and change, and the client's individual uniqueness. The goal of existential interventions and techniques is to free clients from self-centred neurotic limitations of the will and guilt, to make an active responsible authentic commitment in the world in which they live.

Frankl (1946, 1968, 1978, 1980, 1988, 1997) used the word existential in three different ways. The first way was to denote existence itself, specifically the human mode of living. The second was the meaning of that existence. The third was the striving towards a concrete meaning to personal existence. Frankl (1980) supported the general existential analysis of the meaning of life and death, suffering, work and love. It is this will to meaning that is the focus and goal of his Logo-therapy. Specific techniques help find this meaning. Logo-therapy teaches the capacity of self-detachment and self-transcendence. Human beings are capable of forgetting themselves, giving themselves and reaching out for meaning. The uniquely human dimension of frustration adds to the existential nature of his approach. Frankl's two favourite interventions and techniques were the use of de-reflection and paradoxical intention (examined below). His Logo-therapy is the only existential modality that extends beyond its philosophical position to the development of specific interventions and techniques.

May (1961, 1977, 1983, 1989) describes the interaction of a counsellor and client as taking place in four phases: making contact; establishing rapport; confession and interpretations; and transformation of the personality. Existential psychotherapy utilizes any specific technique in each phase that will assist the patient or client to experience, decide and commit to human encounters which are more joy creating than anxiety creating (May 1983).

Core interventions and techniques

Although humanistic schools largely eschew the concept of techniques as such, it is possible to identify specific types of intervention. Some of these are discussed below.

Warming up, ice-breaking

This is a way of starting a session, specifically used to establish rapport and gather some preliminary information. It is seen as valuable since it tends to help the client feel more relaxed and safe, by starting with a non-threatening or social dialogue. The therapist may therefore ask, as in a casual social conversation, how the client is, or whether there were any difficulties finding the therapist's office, or may make a comment about the weather. This is in contrast to the psychoanalytic approach, which is characterized (if not always accurately) as being more held back, sometimes indeed to heighten tension, rather than to alleviate it as warming up remarks are designed to do.

Unconditional positive regard

Again this is less a technique and more of a concept, principally identified with Rogerian client-centred psychotherapy, referring to the establishment of a special kind of rapport with a client that is intended to help the client to feel fully accepted. The experience of this type of relationship is felt to counter earlier experienced parental relationships that may have left the individual with a negative sense of self-worth and a diminishing or a denial of their own potential. There are four primary ways of communicating unconditional positive regard. The first three are through non-verbal communication. The Rogerian therapist adopts a forward leaning attitude to encourage the client's expression of their thoughts and feelings. The therapist makes appropriate eye contact to communicate listening. The therapist clinician adopts a seating arrangement, which is usually at an oblique angle, and without any other furniture as a barrier. The fourth way is the use of parroting or reflective listening in which the clinician repeats the client's words, but usually phrases them as a question. This is intended to communicate that the therapist is both listening and yet also wants to encourage the client to say more. The clinician will listen and want to hear more clarification.

Illustration

C: I would like to get some help.
T: (*adopting a position which shows interest in the client*) M-hm.
C: I tend to feel a lot of fear and anxiety.
T: A lot of fear and anxiety?
C: So I thought I should talk to somebody about it.
T: To talk to somebody?

Restating

Restating is a form of response, again used especially in Rogerian client-centred psychotherapy, which simply repeats what a client says. This is also known as reflective listening, where the psychotherapist reflects back to the client much that the client has said. This reflection or restating is using the clients words as carefully as possible to assure them they have been heard accurately and to prevent the psychotherapist from projecting their own words or emphasis onto the client's statement. It is also known as mirroring. This type of response provides the client with a slightly different perspective on what they are saying, since they are now hearing their words said to them by the psychotherapist.

Illustration

C: I am afraid.
T: M-hm. You are afraid.

C: I have been afraid a long time.
T: Afraid a long time.
C: And I do not want to be afraid anymore.
T: (*expressed with conviction and agreement*) You do not want to be afraid anymore.

Empathy

The major characteristic of humanistic-existential psychotherapy is the use of empathy within a genuine human interaction or encounter in the present experience of the psychotherapeutic relationship. It represents a special focus for the therapist's interventions. Rollo May (1989) defines empathy as the key to the counselling process. The empathic intervention should not be with sympathy, where one person expresses their obvious concern for another. The therapist's concern is to make an identification with the client, which shows how the therapist has understood what the client might be feeling, and through the therapist's ability to tune in to what the client is feeling, to help the therapist to gain a better understanding of the client's experience.

Illustration

C: I just cannot see living this way anymore.
T: I agree. I would not either. (*This is sympathy, rather than empathy.*)
C: So do you see what I am saying?
T: It's very important to you that I should understand what you are feeling. (*This is empathy.*)
C: Wouldn't you feel the same way?
T: You really need to know that you aren't alone.

Authentic therapeutic encounter

Dr Adrian Van Kaam (1966) takes this type of intervention further, with his concept of the authentic therapeutic encounter. The chief characteristic of this is to provide an answer to the appeal of the client. This appeal tells the psychotherapist that the client needs the psychotherapist in a very personal way in this phase of their life development. By authentic, Van Kaam means that the response to the client's appeal should not just come from the intellectualizations of the psychotherapist, but should be a response from the presence of the whole person. To do this, the psychotherapist must be willing to leave their self-centred world of daily involvement and simply be with the client. It is this sense of presence in the psychotherapist, paying attention strictly to the client, that makes the therapist's response both authentic and therapeutic. The unconditional relationship based in the present helps liberate the client from the past to become more creative towards the future. To foster a relationship for optimal communication, a therapeutic attitude of flexibility, acceptance, gentleness and sincerity are important. It is difficult to illustrate this genuine and deep concern without appearing banal, since much of what the therapist conveys is done in their tone of voice.

Awareness continuum

An awareness continuum is in many ways very similar to free association in the psychodynamic or psychoanalytic schools of psychotherapy. The primary difference is that the therapist asks the client to make a series of statements about what they are aware of now in the present tense, as opposed to what they are thinking about. This is an excellent intervention to use to establish rapport, to overcome an impasse or to facilitate a deeper awareness of an experience. Each sentence can begin with 'now', 'at this moment', or 'here and now' (Perls *et al.* 1951). This helps the client to establish contact with what is happening to them and to experience their continuous flow or process of awareness. One such technique requires a client only to report on their body sensations as opposed to any intellectual content.

Illustration

> *C:* So where do I start?
> *T:* What are you aware of now?
> *C:* I am aware that just talking about it makes me fearful.
> *T:* And what are you aware of now?
> *C:* I am aware that my body is getting warmer and my heart is beating faster.
> *T:* And what are you aware of now? . . . etc.

Feedback in the I-Thou

Buber's (1974) I-Thou relationship can be seen as a psychotherapeutic technique whereby the psychotherapist relates the immediacy of his or her own personal inner experience to the client. This is intended to promote a genuine dialogue between client and therapist that is mutually accepting and non-exploitative.

Similarly, Carl Rogers (1977) believes that the release of the individual's capacity for understanding and management of their life comes from a psychological climate in which the psychotherapist is genuine, congruent or real. He advocates psychotherapists being themselves in the relationship without hiding behind a professional front or personal façade. Others refer to this characteristic as being transparent.

Illustration

> *C:* I don't know what to say next.
> *T:* And I don't know either.
> *C:* (*blandly*) OK then, I'll just sit here in silence.
> *T:* Now I am losing focus. I don't experience any energy here at this point.
> *C:* (*responding with feeling*) That makes me angry.
> *T:* Now you have my attention. I'm feeling engaged with you now. Can you say more about that?

Clarification of feelings

It is very characteristic of the humanistic approach to psychotherapy to emphasize feelings, so that a common question is likely to be, 'How do you feel about that?' The more client-centred end of the spectrum in humanistic psychotherapy is content to ask about any feelings associated with what the client is talking about. A gestalt therapist may want to clarify the feelings by offering a possible reframing, such as guilt really being anger directed at one's self, or anxiety as actually being about the fear of excitement.

Closely related to the need to clarify feelings is the technique of affective listening. Affective listening is like reflective listening but takes it one step further, feeding back the perceived affect, emotion or feeling that the clinician *perceives* in the client. The client can then clarify and correct such an observation.

Illustration

    C: What do you want me to say? That I am angry?
    T: I hear what you are saying. Yet, you do not sound angry to me.
    C: I guess it really is not anger that I am feeling.
    T: You sound to me as though you are really frustrated.
    C: I guess I am. I just feel frustrated.
    T: OK, now can you tell me more about that feeling?

Confrontation

To facilitate and to model honesty for the client, the therapist has to be willing to raise difficult issues for the client in order for the client to become more aware of these issues and begin to express more about them. The therapist confronts without aggressive or hostile intent, but from a position of positive regard for the client and genuine concern for their potential: the rationale for the use of confrontation is to make it therapeutic.

Illustration

    C: It is frustrating. I don't know what I am afraid of.
    T: I think you do.
    C: No I don't.
    T: Yes you do. Come on, what are you afraid of right now?
    C: I don't know.
    T: Yes you do. Just say the first thing that comes into your mind.

Deflection or de-reflection

Victor Frankl (1946) noted that when too much attention, or reflection, is given to a problem this attention becomes a problem in itself. The hyper-intention and hyper-reflection becomes a cyclical self-perpetuating reinforcement pattern.

Problems can also be perpetuated and reinforced through hyper-discussion and hyper-interpretation. Therefore, the therapist directs the client to pay attention to something else. This technique takes the excess of attention and puts it on some other object. This is similar to distraction techniques.

Illustration

> C: But I can't think what more to say about my fears. I'm just getting more frightened thinking about it.
> T: OK, sometimes directing too much attention or energy to these things just further creates and perpetuates the problems. So for the moment, let us not waste time by focusing on your fear. Let us find something else to focus on for now.

Existential will and response ability

Dr Van Kaam, in *The Art of Existential Counseling* (1966), offers new insights and techniques into existential will and responsibility. He noticed that many clients entered psychotherapy without a sense of personal will or will power. They felt as if they were victims of other's will or some other generic world force over which they had no power or control. Their lives, in essence, were not their own, so they had no responsibility for what they did or what happened to them in the world. This technique focuses the client back on their own will and their ability to respond to their world by making new decisions and choices.

Illustration

> T: OK then, who is responsible for your fear?
> C: I do not know. I think I have always had it.
> T: So you have always been the victim of your fear?
> C: Yes, it feels that way.
> T: Perhaps that is what you are afraid of the most. You feel that you have no personal power over this fear. Without personal power or responsibility you cannot take charge of your fear and get over it.
> C: That is what I am afraid of.

Gestalt dream-work

Gestalt dream-work is different from traditional psychoanalytical interpretation of dreams. In gestalt dream-work the client is asked and encouraged to 'be' each part of the dream, since the gestalt therapist believes that each part of the dream is a disowned part of the client requiring expression. It is the awareness brought through the expression and owning of these parts that effects healing. Dream interpretation can only be made from the client's own perspective and personal history.

Illustration

> *T:* Does your fear show up in other ways?
>
> *C:* Yes, I am often afraid in my dreams. Something chases me.
>
> *T:* There are several parts to your dream. Each part represents a disowned part of yourself. I want you to become a part of the dream, any part that stands out to you. Let yourself be and express yourself as that part.
>
> *C:* I am running and running and running, but I never get anywhere.
>
> *T:* How do you feel now?
>
> *C:* That old familiar fear.
>
> *T:* Now select the other part of the dream and let yourself be that part.
>
> *C:* I am chasing myself, but I never seem to catch up. I am lost and left behind. I know I scare that part of me, but me as the person chasing is also afraid.

Narrative story telling

The client's experience is a life story that can change with the retelling of it. The client accepts responsibility for the telling of that story and making sense of the story line. By altering, redefining or re-interpreting their life experiences, the client is able to tell a more meaningful story.

Mutual story telling is a method of therapeutic communication, especially appropriate for working with children, which was developed by Richard Gardner (1986). The technique is relatively simple. First, the psychotherapist elicits a story from the child. This enables the psychotherapist to gain valuable insight into the child's inner world, their conflicts, etc. The therapist then creates and tells a story using the same characters and setting, but introducing healthier themes and problem resolutions.

Illustration

>   *T:* There is always a story to tell. This is your life. Tell me your story as if it were a drama.
>
>   *C:* Oh, this is a very sad tragedy . . .
>
>   *T:* OK, now tell me your story as if it were a comedy or a romance story.
>
>   *C:* Well yes, I am like a dog running away from and chasing his own tail at the same time . . .
>
>   *T:* As you told your two stories, which felt the best?
>
>   *C:* Well, the comedy felt better. Like I had some hope I could wake up and quit running away from myself.

Paradoxical intention

Frankl (1946) in his book *Man's Search for Meaning,* offers a technique called paradoxical intention. Fear brings about that which one is afraid of, and prevents one from escaping from it; and the hyper-intention makes impossible what one wishes. Paradoxical intention is used to bring up intentionally that which one is afraid of, so that one can escape it. By this technique, 'the wind is taken out of the sails of the anxiety' (Frankl 1946: 147). One element of Frankl's approach to paradoxical intention is deliberately evoked humour.

Frankl (1978) further saw a cycle of symptoms, evoked, provoked and reinforced. Fear becomes the fear of fear, anxiety becomes anxiety about anxiety, and so on. This develops into a phobic or obsessive-compulsive pattern. The cycle then becomes one where a feeling is induced, followed by resistant counter-pressure, which increases and adds more pressure, further inducing the unwanted symptom.

Illustration

>   *T:* I want to encourage you to do the very thing you are afraid of.

C: Run away from myself?

T: Yes, let's be afraid and run away right now.

C: OK, but I have to warn you. I am very practiced and good at this.

T: OK, since you are going to be afraid anyway, I want you to do your best at being afraid. In fact, let us both compete for who can be the most afraid right now.

Role-playing techniques

Role-playing is one of the most widely used interventions or techniques in the humanistic-existential school of psychotherapy. Role-playing facilitates the awareness and expression of feelings from many possible perspectives and brings the feelings into here-and-now experience.

Gestalt psychotherapy refers to the use of 'experiments' (Polster and Polster 1973: 237) within the therapeutic context. These experiments are usually interventions or techniques such as enactment, directed behaviour, fantasy, dreams and homework. Enactments are of unfinished situations from the distant past, contemporary situations, characteristics, or polarities, meaning the opposites.

Enactment or act-fulfilment are other words for role-playing. Enactment is the process of making something into an act. This can be to take some thought and put some body expression to it through movement and behaviour. The patient or client is encouraged to act out their feelings as long as it does not endanger themselves or any one else. A client stating they feel like crying is encouraged to allow the tears to come. The client may be encouraged to shout or hit a pillow. It can also involve acting a situation out in the psychotherapeutic setting, one that is causing problems in the outside world context.

Illustration

T: To get a better experience of what you are talking about, I would like you to enact the situation right here and right now.

C: Like stand up and start running around the office?

T: Yes, exactly. Get up, run away from yourself and chase yourself at the same time.

C: (*Gets up and runs around the office.*)

The gestalt two-chair or empty chair is another well-known and well-used technique. The therapist asks the client to sit opposite an empty chair, imagining that in the empty chair there sits another person, or a part of themselves, with whom they are experiencing some conflict or trouble. The therapist then encourages the client to speak directly to the empty chair and say whatever they are experiencing. Then the therapist asks the client to physically change chairs and respond from the other position, as if they were the other person, or another part of themselves.

Illustration

> *T:* Now, what would you say to that person chasing you, if they were right here, right now? Put them in that empty chair and tell them how you feel.
> *C:* I am so afraid of you. I want you to stop chasing me. Just stop it.
> *T:* Now, go over and actually sit in that chair and respond back to yourself.
> *C:* I want to stop chasing you. But I can't unless you stop running away from me.
> *T:* Tell him who you feel is running away from you.

To develop an empathic understanding of others, as well as to see one's self from another's perspective, a client may be asked and encouraged to role-play other people in a relationship that is giving them difficulty. Another application is to ask and encourage the client to take the exact opposite position to the one they state they are feeling – obvious feelings often contain their opposite, hidden away. People can miss their full potential by only expressing one half of themselves, the half of which they are consciously aware.

Illustration

> *C:* I feel like my parents ran away from me.
> *T:* How do you feel they experienced you? I'd like you to try being your parents for a few moments. Sit in the chair and speak to your chair, as if you were them.
> *C:* (*as the parents*) We had to go to work for such long hours. We never had any money. We feel bad we didn't spend more time with you and your sisters.

T: (addressing the client as himself, back in his own chair) What are you aware of as you hear their perspective on things?

The client can be encouraged to role-play projections, retrospections and introjections. Projection is the process of denying an aspect of one's self and pushing it away and onto another, like a movie is projected onto a screen (see the companion volume in this series, *Transference and Projection*.) Retroflection is the opposite of projection in which others project onto the client. Introjection is to take the material that has been projected from another and internalize it, as if it was only one's own (see the companion volume in this series, *Internalization*). The technique used here consists of identifying what the client has introjected or projected and reversing the direction.

Illustration

    C: I guess I thought they were running away from me. Yet, I was still afraid.
    T: So you projected your fear on to them?
    C: Apparently. They just felt bad about themselves.
    T: You felt bad about yourself too.
    C: I guess I learned it from them.

To gain from a fuller experience and to expand their awareness, clients can explore and express the opposite or reverse of their current feelings.

Illustration

    T: You say you feel afraid. But I'd like to expand your awareness of what you can feel. Become the opposite of afraid for a few moments.
    C: I feel strong.
    T: How does that feel?
    C: Great.

The client can be encouraged to role-play the different parts of their own self, since the humanistic-existentialist approach views the person as a whole. But it can be useful to draw on an image of the person as being composed of many parts and so to allow the client to express the conflict between different views and feelings. Understanding that they may have parts of them that are in opposition can help the client understand their inner struggle and the stresses caused by this. In gestalt work the therapist asks and encourages the client or patient to play each part, to create a dialogue between them and to find some agreed resolution.

Illustration

> *C:* I have many mixed feelings right now.
> *T:* Mixed feelings are just feelings that come from different parts of you. It sounds like they're not working together. Put one part of yourself on one of your hands and one on the other. Have them talk to each other.
> *C:* One part says 'Stop running'. The other part says 'Stop chasing'. One says 'Stop!', and the other says 'Stop!'
> *T:* Feel your hands as different parts of you and the way they are pulling you in opposite directions. How does that feel?
> *C:* Like it pulls me apart.
> *T:* Now bring those two parts together in front of you. Pull them towards each other, towards you. How does that feel?
> *C:* Like I do not have to feel so split.

Two of the favourite parts that can be role-played in gestalt psychotherapy are top-dog and under-dog. These represent the stereotypical offender-victim dichotomy within the human psyche and in life experience. Few people have a full awareness of or can give full expression to these two conflicted parts of their own being. The top-dog/under-dog technique in gestalt therapy is a means to identify and express opposite sides of any issue. Conflicts can be seen as coming from two opposing forces, and by first identifying these different forces the client can then enact, or become, exaggerate or downplay the two sides in the conflict in an attempt to resolve it.

Illustration

> *C:* I feel like I have been beating myself up over this.
> *T:* Then play the top-dog, the one beating you up.
> *C:* 'You stupid fool. Quit running and hiding from everything.'

T: Now, play the under-dog, the one being beaten up.
C: 'But I am afraid of you.'
T: How do you feel now? What are you aware of?
C: Well, what I can see is that I am playing both these parts all the time.

Role-playing a future situation can also greatly enhance the awareness and expression of the affects that are surrounding it even now. While traditional psychotherapy focuses on the past, and most humanistic work focuses on the present, it is often useful to focus on the future. By asking and encouraging a client to look into the future, they can gain valuable insight and possibly some direction to life.

One gestalt technique is to encourage a client to go forward in time to some future point, perhaps even their death. They then step into, or associate with that experience. This facilitates the ability to find out what might result from any 'unfinished business' that is still around for the client. They may dialogue with others from a future tense projected position. Any insight and awareness that comes from this can then be brought back into the present and integrated into awareness of the current context. One common situation is to role-play a deathbed scenario. The client is encouraged to role-play laying on their deathbed or in their coffin and be aware of their experience and that of the people left behind. The therapist asks the client to identify anything that appears unfinished, and which they may regret as being incomplete. The seeds for that future unfinished business are already there in their present life. The experience allows them to finish something so they will not have to experience the continuing pain of it for the rest of their life.

Illustration

T: If you continue to feel this way, what do you feel the future will hold?
C: Like I will go nuts or something. The future doesn't look good.
T: Go into the future, as if you are that future person right here and right now, how do you feel?
  Is there anything the future you wants you to know? Is there anything unfinished that you regret? Tell them right here and right now.
C: (*from the future*) Just relax. Quit beating yourself up. There

is nothing to be afraid of. Life has some struggle and pain to it. That is part of the meaning of life. Just accept it without being afraid of it.

A similarly intentioned technique can be found in 'logo-drama', developed by Viktor Frankl in order to facilitate a patient finding meaning in their life, love and suffering, introduced in his book *Man's Search for Meaning* (1946). This technique allows a client to look at their life, through a process of going ahead in time, and looking back.

Enhancing affective awareness and expression techniques

One of the most frequently used techniques to enhance awareness and expression is to stay with the feeling. An almost paradoxical intervention, the psychotherapist asks and encourages the client to stay with their feelings rather than immediately attempt to avoid them. This allows the client to fully experience their feelings and to learn from them. Claudio Naranjo (1973) notes that the basic prescription is to 'be aware'. One cannot be aware of an experience while one is avoiding it. Therefore, a basic intervention or technique is to stay with the feelings and stop doing anything else. The experience and awareness is of the present, in the here-and-now. Unlike a psychodynamic technique, which may first involve understanding a person's defences (or as Reich would put it, their 'character-armour'), which may be related to past needs to repress feeling, humanistic models prefer to encourage facing feelings from the start.

Illustration

> *T:* Stay with that feeling for a moment.
> *C:* I feel afraid it will not last. It feels strange to think positively about the future.
> *T:* I would like you to stay with the feeling for now. Tell me more.
> *C:* I am afraid to be peaceful.
> *T:* Just stay with the feeling and look at me. Stay with the feeling and stay with me.
> *C:* (*tears*)
> *T:* What are you aware of now?

Repetition of what a client is doing is another useful technique to facilitate enhancement of awareness and expression of feelings. As a means to bring about a fuller awareness and expression of an experience a client may be encouraged to repeat a phrase they have just spoken or a gesture they have just made (Naranjo 1973).

Illustration

> C: I have wasted so much time.
> T: Say that again.
> C: I have wasted so much time. (*shakes head from side to side*)
> T: Say that again and make the same gesture.
> C: I have wasted so much time.
> T: How does that feel?

The exaggeration of an expression, whether verbal or physical, can facilitate and heighten the awareness and expression of that experience. Naranjo (1973) states that to be aware an individual must stop avoiding and bring more energy to bear on the content of awareness through intensified attention and deliberate exaggeration. As an expressive intervention or technique, exaggerating is a call to initiate action and maximize expression in an unstructured situation. If the client states they are 'not' doing or expressing something, the therapist may encourage the client to exaggerate that very thing.

Illustration

> C: I have. I have wasted so much of my life being afraid.
> T: Can you say that louder?
> C: It is a waste of time being afraid.
> T: Can you really exaggerate your gestures as you continue to say it louder?
> C: (*stamps foot*) It is a waste of time being afraid.
> T: What are you experiencing or aware of now?

'Aboutism' and 'shouldism'

When the clients talk 'about' something in a detached manner, they are responding from a dissociated position rather than from the immediacy of awareness of their present experience. Similarly when a client talks about what they 'should' do, or feel, or think, they are expressing an external locus of power and an implied statement about what they do not do, think or feel. These expressions go against the humanistic-existential foundation of self-responsibility and awareness of a present here-and-now experience.

'Aboutism' and 'shouldism' are two of the names given by Fritz Perls in gestalt therapy (Naranjo 1973) for the science and religion 'game'. Perls believes that both 'why' and 'because' are dirty words used to defend and rationalize rather than to experience. Aboutisms are a manipulation or misuse of the intellect, which sacrifice the immediacy of the experience. Gestalt therapists consider generalization, evaluation and interpretation a step or more removed from true awareness.

'Shouldism' refers to rules given by others to control life, not experience it. The usual gestalt challenge to 'shouldism' is to caution people about 'shoulding' all over themselves.

Illustration

> C: I don't even know what it is all about.
> T: I don't want you to tell me 'about': I want you to experience it right here and right now.
> C: I should not be afraid, especially of myself.
> T: Please, do not 'should' on your self.
> C: Oh, I've been very good at 'shoulding' on myself.

Asking takes away one's personal power. It makes the search for meaning the responsibility of another. This also goes against the humanistic-existential position. In gestalt therapy, the client is encouraged not to ask questions or for permission. Gestalt therapists feel that all asking is a demand in disguise. They tell the client to make the question into a personal statement.

Illustration

> C: Do you think that is what this is all about?
> T: Are you asking or telling me?
> C: I guess I was asking.
> T: Then tell me. Make the question into a personal statement from you.

C: This is what it's about: I've wasted my time running away from myself.

T: Now, how does that feel?

Completing or closure

Central to the beliefs of the humanistic-existential school of psychotherapy is the innate drive towards completion. Therefore, anything left 'unfinished' will remain as an internal conflict. This is referred to as 'unfinished business'. The technique of completion is designed to encourage a client to enact previous 'unfinished business' in a way that will allow them to experience a 'finished' awareness of it.

Illustration

T: How do you feel right now?

C: I feel great. Like I don't have to run away from myself any more.

T: Do you feel like everything is completed and finished now?

C: Yes.

T: Then let's stop here.

Doing the rounds

The humanist-existentialist position holds that we are both separate and yet connected to others. This means that in some humanistic models (such as gestalt) the use of a group as the context for therapy is highly desirable. The group gives a better feeling of being in the world. In addition, the reactions, and responses of others in the group, besides the psychotherapist, offer quantity as well as quality to the support of the client.

'Doing the rounds' is a particular gestalt technique mostly used by group and family psychotherapists. It involves going around the group and 'checking in' with each participant.

Illustration

T: Let's start. Let's go around the group. Each person states what he or she is aware of right now and what he or she would like today from this experience.

OK. Who wants to work? (*one member indicates she wishes to go first*)

OK. Go around the group and tell each person what you are aware of right here and now.

Other expressive experientially-active techniques and modalities

Another set of techniques is included here for comparison. These techniques are largely humanistic in outlook, yet behaviourist in method and place much more emphasis on non-verbal communication, although some techniques, such as certain forms of art therapy or psycho-drama, or play therapy, are practiced in a variety of modalities, including both person centred and psychoanalytic.

Philosophically the expressive and experiential styles of psychotherapy share more with the humanists and existentialists. A client brings in an expression that is accepted and appreciated within the therapeutic relationship and context. The client then enters a deeper inner experiencing by 'being' and expressing it. Expressive and experiential psychotherapies believe that personal growth comes from any expression or experience that brings about awareness, and that this sustains or directs personal change. This style of psychotherapy is included under the behavioural section because the client or individual demonstrates these expressions or experiences on a behavioural level in a behavioural way.

Art therapy

Adrian Hill originally coined the expression 'art therapy' in 1942. Art therapy (Waden 1980; Rubin 1984, 1987, 1999) uses a wide range of visual art material, especially drawing and painting as a means of expression. Art, throughout history, has been an expression of individual perception and feeling. The emphasis here is on a form of communication that is initially expressive and non-verbal. Clients, who may or may not be able to express themselves in words, are encouraged instead to express themselves through art. Children are especially adept at engaging in art therapy, as they are in play. An art therapist may ask a client to draw a picture of their family. The size, location, colours and proximity to each other will provide many clues to how the individual actually experiences their family. Some therapists also use stones or other small objects with a similar purpose; of identifying family members and their relative distance from each other. The inner experience of the client thus finds external expression. This form of physical expression, first produced just through movement, paint, handling of objects, can then become the subject of interpretation – which will take many forms, depending on the clinical orientation of the therapist. It may be analysed for psychodynamic unconscious conflicts or simply used for encouraging the verbal expression of the feelings that accompanied the action of painting, use of colour, etc. The humanistic approach particularly favours the individual client interpreting their work idiosyncratically, using their own frame of reference. Art may also be used (as in psychosynthesis) to express and promote underlying awareness of more transpersonal spiritual themes.

Dance therapy

Dance psychotherapy (Rosen 1957; Schoop 1974; Espenak 1981; Levy 1988; Exiner 1994) is the therapeutic application of movement, where rhythm and physical expression permits both the flowing of inner feelings, but also identification of blocks to feeling. Research indicates that rhythm and emotion imprint in the same right hemisphere of the brain. Dance permits exploration of feelings throughout the body, and expression of the whole person. Rituals using movement, music and rhythm appear throughout time and across cultures, promoting group and individual well-being. In dance therapy participants are encouraged to dance in a way that expresses what they feel or think, or which portrays some issue that troubles them. The therapist may then ask the participants to express in dance how they would like to feel, think or behave.

Music psychotherapy

Music has, similarly, had therapeutic value throughout time and across cultures (Meyers 1961; Seashore 1967; Mursell 1971; Hargreaves 1986; Hodges 1996). There is research evidence that the beat and rhythm can help synchronize with brain waves and directly affect the functioning of the brain. An example would be listening to slower (60 beats per minutes) music during times of anxiety. Sixty beats per minutes is also the rate of beta waves in the brain that corresponds to a relaxed state. Research also suggests that this slower music can also aid learning. Music psychotherapy was very popular in psychiatric hospitals and universities during the 1940s and 1950s (Alvin 1979).

Music is another right hemispheric function, a very direct way to access emotional states. The therapist also uses music as a diagnostic tool. The music a person listens to gives some clue as to their personality.

Play psychotherapy

Play therapy (Axline 1969; James 1969; Schaefer 1994a, b; O'Conner 1997) is clearly useful with children since it is developmentally their natural means of expression. Play is the language of childhood and it becomes a window that allows a psychotherapist to see into the child's world. It provides an expression for both imagination and fantasy, a release of energy and a context for social learning, creativity and the practicing of new physical skills.

Play therapy can be seen as an extension of psychoanalytic theory applied to children (Klein 1932; Freud 1946). Anna Freud learned some of her techniques from Montessori. Play therapy is used in many other modalities, particularly person-centred work. Setting limits is important as the play therapist allows the child full expression of their feelings and fantasies. The therapist may be passive and use observation for diagnostic assessment, or may interact with the child in a kind of dialogue, using words and action to access further feelings, or perhaps to offer a new direction, to provide insight or suggest a different kind of behaviour. The toys used in play therapy can range from those specifically designed for play therapy such as anatomically correct dolls, to the usual material found in the child's room at home.

In a humanistic orientation, the goal of play therapy is just to increase awareness and expression. Violet Oaklander (1978) offers many valuable tools for clinicians practicing this form of play therapy. Although it is sometimes thought that play therapy is only used with children, it can also be an invaluable tool for the facilitation of regression for adults suffering from childhood trauma.

Primal psychotherapy

Arthur Janov (1970, 1972, 1980, 1991, 1996) developed primal therapy in the 1960s. Its focus is on the vivid re-experiencing of early infancy and childhood pain. This re-experiencing is referred to as a 'primal'. Its full expression is often in an intense scream. Primal therapy demonstrates neurosis in reverse. Janov believes that neurosis is the product of blocked expression of childhood pain. The expression of that pain in the form of a deep primal scream can unblock the energy that is fixated. Primal therapy deals with a direct expression of the feelings in the form of regression, not through words or talking about an earlier painful situation.

Psychodrama

Psychodrama, developed by Jacob L. Moreno (1946, 1959, 1975) during the 1930s, is a group psychotherapy in which clients act out those situations that cause them difficulty, in the present and from the past. The purpose is to engage in action and dialogue that will uncover unconscious material and promote insight into the situation the client brings. There are close links to the psychodynamic school. The context of psychodrama also enables the rehearsing of new behaviours.

Psychodrama is a technique to externalize the internal world of the client. The enactment usually takes place on a stage. The 'client' will choose others from the group to play certain roles in their re-enactment. The 'client', as the main character in the play, tells others how to play their roles, and briefs them as to what they might want to say. This method allows the 'client' to re-experience the situation that they bring within a safe context. The group leader and the client may act like a director in the theatre, offering direction and feeding lines to the players. The individual may play the central figure in their drama, the protagonist, but at other times, it may be useful to have the individual play another role to get insight into other players in his or her drama. Usually the group starts with a warm-up time, followed by the staging of the drama and de-briefing – a very important part of the process.

Summary and conclusions

In conclusion, what these different methods of therapy have in common is that they stress awareness and genuine expression of feelings, present experience and process. Some of what has been described should perhaps not be called technique as such, since the emphasis is on the quality of the relationship between therapist and client. The humanistic-existential schools tend to look unfavourably on therapists who appear more to be technicians than creators of an authentic, even artistic, experience. Therapists in the humanistic-existential school tend to trust their intuition and 'guts', heart more than head, feeling more than cognitive thought.

So, beyond the interventions and techniques, Carl Rogers (1961) emphasizes the qualities of the helping relationship: that the therapist should be trustworthy, dependable and consistent; must be able to communicate unambiguously, to express a positive attitude of warmth, caring, liking, interest and respect towards the other person. The therapist must be secure in their respect for their own feelings and needs, whilst keeping them separate from those of the client, so that they will not be perceived as a threat. The therapist must be willing and able to enter fully and accept the other's world of experience, being and meaning without evaluating the other's unique process of becoming. It is this combination of positive regard, acceptance and empathic understanding by the psychotherapist that is healing, not psychotherapeutic interventions and techniques.

May (1983) thinks that western culture believes understanding follows from technique. The existential school of psychotherapy holds the opposite as true, that techniques flow from understanding. The goal of the psychotherapist is to understand the client as a unique being in his or her unique world. Without this understanding of existing and existence, technical proficiency is irrelevant to the central process of psychotherapy.

Rogers (1961) believes that psychotherapy is a process which involves learning. The client learns to move from symptoms to themselves, from the environment to themselves, from others to themselves, from the past to the present and from the negative to the positive.

But if the humanistic-existential school only uses interventions and techniques to facilitate the awareness and expression of feelings, other schools have a very different emphasis. The next developmental stage of psychotherapy places its emphasis on thoughts and cognitions, and it is this that is examined in the next chapter.

C H A P T E R 5

Cognitive psychotherapy and cognitive-behavioural psychotherapy

If the development of some of the different schools of therapy is traced, an evolutionary shift from one form to another is found: the behaviour therapy movement developed as a response and reaction to the psychodynamic school; the humanistic-existential movement developed as a response and reaction to the behaviourist school; and the cognitive movement developed as a response and reaction to the humanistic-existential school. Insight and the significance of the past gave way to behavioural learning theory; this in turn was followed by more emphasis on feelings; and this has shifted in cognitive therapy to a different focus on the thinking processes.

Cognition is the process of knowing or perceiving, for example, an idea. Cognitive psychotherapy is an active, directive, time-limited, structured approach where the theoretical rationale is that affect, feelings and behaviour are largely determined by the way a person constructs or thinks about the world. The important cognitions are views of self, the future and the world. These thoughts or cognitions are based on assumptions or schema developed earlier in life, some of which are distorted. It is therefore thoughts, beliefs and attitudes, and the questioning of assumptions, that are the primary unit of this form of therapy. Beliefs (Dryden and Golden 1987) take many forms. They present as non-evaluative observations or inferences, and positive or negative preferential evaluations. Major techniques for disputing irrational beliefs are debating, discriminating and defining. The core rationale for cognitive psychotherapeutic interventions and techniques is the identification and disputing of *negative* schema, beliefs or cognitive errors.

Cognitive techniques are important but only as part of a more general cognitive strategy of assessment within a therapeutic relationship. The inner-directed information processing about the self and the world emphasizes a logical consistent view of human nature.

There are different forms of cognitive and cognitive-behavioural techniques (Kendall and Hollan 1979), which are illustrated here through some of the most well known. Cognitive methods include self-examination, explanation, self-demonstration and modelling (Mahoney and Freeman 1985). Cognitive-behavioural methods include alternative thinking, contingency contracting and management, covert or internal conditioning, modelling, rehearsal, response cost, sensitization, imagery, self-statements and verbalizations. The foundation of cognitive-behaviour psychotherapeutic interventions and techniques (Foreyt and Rathjen 1978) is the disputing of irrational beliefs. Other interventions and techniques can include identifying cognitive distortion patterns by making double and triple columns of unreasonable thinking, reasonable thinking and reinterpretation.

Cognitive-behavioural psychotherapy is based on the theory that a stimulus event is cognitively processed, which may result in physiological arousal and/or a subjective feeling state. This leads to impulses to action and overt behaviour that have the effect of satisfying a motive or of adapting to circumstances in ways that promote survival (Dryden and Golden 1987: 9). Cognitions contain symbolic representation, misconception hypotheses, errors in logic, predictions, post-dictive conclusions, irrational beliefs, automatic thoughts, feelings, and self and other cognitions. Assessment strategies (Kendall and Hollan 1981) encompass attribution styles, belief systems, self-referent speech, imagery, therapeutically relevant motivation and interpersonal problem-solving skills.

Aaron Beck (Beck and Emery 1979) was one of the first to dispute systematically irrational thoughts as a means of psychotherapeutic interventions. He identified three common irrational beliefs, and challenges. *Re-attribution* challenges the assumptions of blame by considering alternative causes of an event. *De-centring* challenges the assumption that the client is the centre of attention and continuously vulnerable to other people's judgements. *De-catastrophizing* challenges the 'what if?' or 'what would happen if the worst case scenario occurred with? . . . and then what?' Beck states that the overall strategy for cognitive therapy centres on a 'collaborative enterprise' (Arkowitz 1989) that explores and modifies distorted and unrealistic meanings. A second strategy is a guided discovery of themes and beliefs in the client's current experience. But Beck cautioned cognitive therapists not to become so enamoured of techniques that they lost sight of the therapeutic relationship.

Re-attribution

A client may attribute their anger to what someone else said or did. It was the other person who caused them to get angry. The cognitive psychotherapist challenges how the other person caused the anger. The therapist guides the client to understand that it was their own thought about the other person, or what they themselves said or did, which actually caused the anger. If they had thought about it differently, they may not have got angry. Cognitive psychotherapy thus challenges the validity, reality, or usefulness of these types of cause and effect relations.

De-catastrophizing

De-catastrophizing is a technique that challenges the reality or probability of catastrophic consequences.

Illustration

> T: If your parents, the world and God hated you, what do you think would happen?
> C: That I would spend the rest of my life alone.
> T: Seems like you pretty well have.
> C: Yes . . . which convinced me it was true.
> T: What is the probability of your parents, the world and God hating you?
> C: Well, the probability is small.
> T: What is the probability of living your life alone?
> C: That I have been good at getting. The probability is high.

Decentring

The intervention or a technique of decentring facilitates the natural maturation process of the client realizing that she or he is not the centre of everything.

Illustration

> *T:* So, the probability is high that you will live your life alone?
> *C:* Seems like it.
> *T:* You believe the probability is high that you will be alone because your parents, the world and God hate you?
> *C:* Yes.
> *T:* You believe that your parents, the world and God have singled you out and spend all their time just making sure you will live alone?
> *C:* Well, I did not actually say that.
> *T:* You seem to believe that you have been singled out as the centre of all this attention just for the sole purpose of keeping you alone. You must feel important to believe you deserve all this attention.
> *C:* I do not feel that important.
> *T:* Then perhaps no one singled you out to be doomed to anger, depression and to live alone.
> *C:* That would be a great way to think.

Cognitive restructuring

Cognitive restructuring or reframing is one of the most important contributions of the cognitive school of psychotherapy. Cognitive restructuring is a psychotherapeutic technique that helps people recognize and change unwanted thoughts leading to a poor self-concept or to maladaptive or self-defeating behaviours. The client first becomes aware of the self-deprecating, illogical or irrational thoughts in the statements they believe and make about themselves. They then substitute positive statements. Re-defining is similar, involving giving new meaning to the same situation.

Many means can be utilized to accomplish cognitive restructuring. The psychotherapist may use didactic explanations, Socratic dialogue or questioning, corrective experiences, vicarious learning, self-analysis, self-statement modification, mental rehearsal, reframing by changing the meaning, story telling/metaphors/poetry, cognitive paradox by exaggerating the voice of irrationality and teaching problem-solving skills (Dryden and Golden 1987: 359–61).

Illustration

> *T:* Do you believe that other people are worthy of love?
> *C:* Yes.

T: Everyone?

C: Yes.

T: Everyone except you?

C: Well.

T: Right. We have already established that the critical parent and hurt child in your head are just the perceptions you had of your parents. That perception may not be real or right. We have attributed your thinking to only your thinking, not who you are or your generic worth. We have established that you are not important enough to be the centre of everyone's, including God's, sole attention. So the rule of the reality you have been living with, does not appear to be anything more than a set of misperceptions and irrational beliefs. So, what would you have to believe to let go of your anger and depression?

C: That it is not all about me.

T: Anything else?

C: That I do not have to be perfect to have love.

T: That sounds good too.

Bridging and tracking

Bridging (Dryden and Golden 1987) refers to tuning into a client's preferred representational system before branching off to another area. Tracking (Dryden and Golden 1987) is the careful scrutinizing of the BASIC-ID, which is described below. It is the [psychotherapeutic] process of following a client's thought until they arrive at the core maladaptive belief or cognition. A common question used in tracking is, 'and if that happened?' Tracking follows the client's own thinking until they discover some underlying, usually unknown, belief about their own worth.

BASIC-ID

Two ways of working, which use acronyms – perhaps illustrating the way in which cognitive therapies try to make their approaches more readily understandable, appealing to more straightforward thinking in the client – are now described. BASIC-ID (Dryden and Golden 1987) is the first of these acronyms, setting out a plan of therapeutic action for cognitive-behavioural therapy:

B Behaviour extinction, counter-conditioning positive reinforcement, punishment
A Affective abreaction, owning and accepting feeling
S Sensations in the physical body, tension release and sensory pleasuring
I Images to change in self-image
C Cognitive restructuring
I Interpersonal modelling and relationships
D Diagnosis of and intervention in medical conditions

Illustration

T: What are some of the behaviours that accompany your anger and depression?

C: I tend to be really short-tempered and impatient with everyone and everything.

T: What are the feelings that accompany your anger and depression?

C: I feel awful all the time. Again, just angry and sad.

T: What are the physical sensations you experience accompanying your anger and depression?

C: I swing from being very tense and nervous to being angry and depressed.

T: What are the images that accompany your anger and depression?

C: I just keep replaying past failures in my head.

T: What are the thoughts that accompany your anger and depression?

C: The critical parent yelling and the hurt child crying, as we said before.

T: What happens in your interpersonal relationships because of your anger and depression?

C: What interpersonal relationships? It seems the only relationship I have is in my head between the critical parent and the hurt child.

T: Are there any medical conditions that could account for your anger and depression?

C: I have not had a complete medical physical examination for a while. I will get one just to see if there is anything. I do not think there is. I am healthy.

Rational Emotive Therapy

One of the major contributors to cognitive psychotherapy is Albert Ellis and his Rational Emotive Therapy (Ellis 1962, 1973, 1985, 1988; Ellis and Harper 1975; Ellis and Grieger 1986; Ellis and Dryden 1987) and later termed Rational Emotive Behavior Therapy (REBT). The goal of REBT is similarly to show the client their irrational beliefs and to help them adopt ones that are more rational. This form of therapy has further developed the idea that one feels what one thinks. REBT also uses an acronym, the easily remembered ABC. A is for the activating event, the B for the beliefs about the activating event, and C for the consequential response. The ABC principle states that between the activating event and external stimulus A, and the end response or cognitive, affective and behavioural consequence C, is the individual's belief system B. To feel well one must think straight. In the therapy, the therapist is very active and persuasive, although Ellis (Dryden and Golden 1987) emphasizes the need to accept unconditionally, to be therapeutically genuine, to show appropriate humour and to demonstrate philosophic empathy.

The strategy in the session (Dryden and Golden 1987: Ch 5) follows a prescribed sequence. First, the psychotherapist checks on the completion of any homework assigned. This is followed by enquiries about the most pressing problem. The psychotherapist then helps the client to see the relationship between irrational beliefs and evaluative conclusions, and to dispute irrational 'must-urbatory' beliefs. The therapist would also encourage the client to dispute, continually, irrational and distorted beliefs outside of session. They negotiate homework, continuing to identify and dispute distorted inferences.

The ABC theory of Rational Emotive Behaviour Therapy

The fear of failure and the need for approval are two commonly held, yet limiting and irrational, beliefs. Individuals can make positive or negative preferential or 'musturbatory' evaluations. Most irrational beliefs fall into one of the following categories: all or nothing thinking, jumping to conclusions, fortune-telling, focusing on the negative, disqualifying the positive, 'all-ness' or 'never-ness', minimizing, emotional reasoning, labelling or overgeneralizing, personalizing, 'phony-ism', and perfectionism. Psychological health in REBT includes self-interest, social interest, self-direction, high frustration tolerance, flexibility, acceptance of uncertainty, scientific thinking, self-acceptance, risk-taking, long-range hedonism or pleasure seeking, non-utopianism and self-responsibility for own emotional disturbances. The therapist facilitates distinctions between concern and anxiety, sadness and expression, regret and guilt, disappointment and shame or embarrassment, and annoyance and anger.

Therapeutic change comes about from a number of factors. All interventions and techniques focus toward these ends. The first is realizing that one creates one's own disturbances. Clients need to recognize their ability to change significantly that disturbance. They develop and demonstrate an understanding that the disturbances come from irrational dogmatic beliefs. The therapy focuses on detecting and disputing irrational beliefs. Finally, the individual begins to internalize new beliefs and continue the process of challenging the irrational beliefs.

Identification of and disputing irrational beliefs

Ellis has delineated several common irrational beliefs:

1 the necessity for love and approval;
2 the belief that one must be thoroughly competent, adequate, and achieving in all possible respects;
3 certain people are bad and should be blamed and punished;
4 it is terrible when things are not as I want them;
5 the external cause of all unhappiness;
6 the necessity of preoccupation with that which is fearsome or dangerous;
7 it is easier to avoid difficulties and responsibilities than to accept them;
8 the past is all-important;
9 things should be different than they are;
10 inertia and inaction can only achieve happiness;
11 the need for something greater than our self to rely on.

Albert Ellis (Dryden and Golden 1987) developed a method of disputing irrational beliefs, known as DIBS: a series of questions used therapeutically. They are:

• What beliefs do I want to dispute?
• Can I rationally support this belief?
• What evidence exists of the truth of this belief?
• What evidence exists for the falseness of this belief?

- What are the worse possible things that could happen?
- What good things could happen?

Illustration

> *T:* When does your critical parent start?
>
> *C:* I guess it starts whenever I make a mistake or things do not go just the way I think they should.
>
> *T:* So any external event that does not go the way you think it should will start the critical parent yelling?
>
> *C:* Yes.
>
> *T:* So let us see if we can uncover the beliefs behind that critical parent and that hurt child. Let us see what motivates them. OK?
>
> *C:* OK.
>
> *T:* The critical parent produces your anger. What are they thinking?
>
> *C:* They think I have to be perfect and cannot make mistakes.
>
> *T:* What will happen if the child makes mistakes? What is the worst thing that will happen?
>
> *C:* Well, I think they think they will look like bad parents. I mean I know they are trying to teach me to do my best.
>
> *T:* So, even though you know they come with good intentions, they think it is about them and their need to be seen as good parents. How does the child see it?
>
> *C:* If I am not perfect, my parents will not love me.
>
> *T:* What evidence do you have that you have to be perfect or that if you are not perfect no one will love you?
>
> *C:* There is no evidence. I am not perfect.
>
> *T:* No one is. What are the consequences you experience in life for having this critical parent and hurt child?
>
> *C:* As you said, anger and depression.
>
> *T:* So, who creates your anger and depression?
>
> *C:* I do.
>
> *T:* So, who can change it?
>
> *C:* I can.

Reality Therapy

While still classified as a cognitive approach, the main principle of Reality Therapy is that personal identity and self-worth develops in 'doing' behaviour that develops responsibility and initiative. Developed by William Glasser (1976, 1989a, 1989b), the therapeutic task begins with the therapist establishing rapport and becoming involved, by asking what behaviour the client is engaged in now. Together they examine or evaluate whether that behaviour is doing any good, whether it is working for the client. If not, they develop a plan that might work. The therapist and client establish a contract and follow it through without accepting excuses, and without any form of judgement. Ongoing evaluation supports a 'never-give-up' attitude. The goal in Reality Therapy is to confront the reality of internalized cognitions that threaten our feeling loved and worthy. The therapy keeps both clinician and client focused on choices the client really does have control over.

William Glasser (1965) saw the basic human needs as relatedness and respect. He advocated health through the three 'R's of reality, responsibility, and right-and-wrong. Healthy individuals live with realistic expectations for themselves and others. They are responsible for demonstrating the ability to fulfil their own needs without depriving others of the ability to fulfil theirs. Healthy individuals know what is right and act on it.

The therapist must model a very responsible person, strong yet never expedient, knowledgeable and understanding in order to develop therapeutic involvement. Reality therapists frequently ask questions such as: What are you doing? Is that in your or your family's best interest? Is it working to get what you want? How will this action help? Due to this questioning on a reality basis, this form of cognitive psychotherapy works very well with clients of more limited intelligence and education.

Illustration

> *T:* So, what are you doing now to accept your imperfections and still let in love?
> *C:* Nothing.
> *T:* Does doing nothing realistically work?
> *C:* No.
> *T:* What might work?
> *C:* Well, if I quit talking to myself that way.
> *T:* How will this action realistically help?
> *C:* I will not talk myself out of trying for fear I will make some mistake.

T: OK. Good. Let's establish a realistic plan. What can you do inside your head and realistically in your life to demonstrate that now you realistically know what is right and what you are responsible for? Can you keep track of this, and then counter the thoughts of the critical parent with some encouragement and support from the adult part of you?

C: That should work.

T: It's a start. I will follow up on your progress next time.

Self-instructional training

Yet another form of cognitive therapy is seen in Donald Meichenbaum's (1977) development of SIT: Self-instructional training, as a means to change the statements clients make to and of themselves. Self-instructional training lends itself to broader categories of interventions in which the client is active in their own self-instruction.

Self-monitoring focuses on affect, behaviour and cognition by observing shifts in moods and the associated thoughts. Behavioural techniques of scheduling, rehearsal and role-playing, self-reliance training, diversion techniques, hypothesis testing and exposure therapy are also used. Besides covert and overt verbalization, images play an important part in cognition and interventions involving images include image thought-stopping with verbalizations of 'stop it', realistic repetition, time projection, metaphors, de-catastrophizing images, induced images, goal rehearsal, positive images and coping images.

Illustration

T: So let us attempt to come up with your own programme to teach yourself that you don't have to yell at yourself with your critical parent. You do not have to be the hurt child. You do not need to believe that everyone in the world and God is against you. Sound good?

C: Yes.

T: Do you believe that it is possible?

C: I do now.

T: In fact, because you have already been so good at getting your feelings and life to respond to your thoughts, we already know your body-mind connection is good. Now we are just

talking about switching the content. What would you have
to think not to have that anger and depression in you?

C: That it is not all about me and I am worthy.

T: Is that the self-talk in your head?

C: Yes.

T: OK. Every time you start thinking like the critical parent,
I would like the adult part of you to come in, interrupt
that thought from yelling at you, and tell yourself it is
not all about you and you are worthy. OK?

C: OK.

T: What image would help you believe that?

C: It would help to have an image of me being happy,
successful and in love. (*Smiles*)

T: OK, hold that image and repeat the self-talk. How does
that feel?

C: Great. (*More smiles*)

T: How would you hold your body and what would you be
doing with these new beliefs?

C: I would hold myself straighter, start working out again and
probably eat a lot better. (*Laughing*)

T: OK. Guess what your homework is?

C: (*Just laughs*)

T: Any questions?

C: No.

Multi-modal therapy

Arnold Lazarus and his technical eclecticism (1971, 1976, 1981, 1985)
stresses a multi-modal approach to psychotherapy. This approach
emphasizes seven factors: behaviour, affect, sensation, imagery,
cognition, interpersonal relationships and biological functioning.
As a multi-modal therapist, Lazarus advocates many types of intervention and techniques as described here and elsewhere, including
medication, imagery, fantasy, Rogerian reflection and the gestalt
empty chair exercise.

Transactional analysis

It may seem strange to include Eric Berne's (1961, 1964, 1972,
1976, 1977) transactional analysis (TA) in a chapter on cognitive

psychotherapy. TA often claims to have more psychodynamic roots than anything else and indeed Berne's background was psychoanalysis. But it is included here because there is a strong element of the analysis of ways of thinking and responding, which are identified as the three ego states of parent, adult and child, each of which has its own scripts. The parent may be controlling or natural and nurturing, and incorporates aspects of our own parents. The child is an ego state that is more archaic and may be rebellious, adaptive or natural. The adult is the ego state that is more directed towards objectivity and autonomy containing the healthy adaptive aspects of the personality. TA also uses a number of terms that help the client to identify their responses and behaviours, such as games, rackets and strokes. The goal of transactional analysis treatment is to facilitate the client's movement from games to intimacy and so to avoid self-destructive scripts. The method uses structural analysis, in which the three ego states (parent, adult and child) undergo analysis within the life script. Games are also identified. The therapist often has an educational role explaining or teaching, as well as interpreting, so that the client is helped to *think* about the way they are in different situations. A contract is agreed with explicit goals, of which the overall goal is to reach a point where the client feels 'OK' about their self and 'OK' about the external social world in which they interact.

Illustration

    T: How can I be of most help to you today?
    C: I am tired of feeling angry and depressed all the time.
    T: So you would be willing to commit to working on your anger and depression?
    C: Yes.
    T: Tell me more about your anger or depression.
    C: I think when I am angry, I am most angry with myself.
    T: When you are angry with your self, how do you do that in your head? Do you talk to yourself?
    C: I would not say talk. It is more like yell.
    T: What do you say?
    C: 'You idiot. You should have known better.'
    T: So you scold yourself, much like a very critical parent?
    C: Exactly.

T: Then after you scold yourself like a critical parent, do you feel like a hurt child?

C: Yes, exactly.

T: When you are angry you are being the critical parent. When you are depressed, you are being the hurt child.

Transactions take place between the parent-adult-child ego states of one person and the parent-adult-child ego states of the other, or within the one person. Trouble often comes in crossed transactions in which communication is broken off because the stimulus of one transaction (adult-adult) produces a crossed or different response (child-parent) in the other. The therapist may illustrate how this miscommunication takes place:

T: Those two roles, the critical parent and the hurt child, complement each other. The one depends on the other. What would happen if, the next time you thought like the critical parent, you respond back from a more adult point of view?

C: Well, I guess that as an adult I would not let anybody talk to me that way.

T: Probably not.

Interactions take different forms: withdrawal, rituals, strokes or work activities. When they become repetitive ulterior transactions with a well-defined psychological pay-off, they become games. The formula for a game consists of the initial 'con', followed by a 'switch', a 'cross-up' and a 'pay-off'. What is important here is to recognize the way the therapist may use these terms to help the client grasp what is happening, and help the client analyse the situation.

T: How do you think the critical parent and the hurt child initially hook or con each other?

C: Well, it is chicken or egg. The hurt child hooks the critical parent by making stupid mistakes. The critical parent hooks the hurt child by first thinking they are coming to the rescue. Then they just yell and make matters worse.

T: So the more mistakes the more yelling and the more yelling the more mistakes?

C: That sounds about right.

T: Go inside and listen. Is it right?

C: Yes that is exactly what they are doing.

According to TA, each person has a preconscious life plan or script. The script is the larger picture of life and is used to structure transactions. Usually these scripts develop their basis in childhood illusions. Many scripts contain childhood decisions or commitments to certain forms of behaviour, which later become the basis of the individual character or personality. We need not describe scripts in detail here, but rather show how they are used in the therapy itself.

T: Have they always done this?
C: As long as I can remember.
T: Where did you learn to do this to yourself?
C: What do you mean?
T: Did you have a critical parent growing up?
C: Oh yes, absolutely. Both of my parents were quick to point out my mistakes.
T: Can you really identify with the hurt child?
C: Yes, it is how I felt growing up.
T: So now you just do it to yourself. You do not need your parents' help anymore. You've got good at repeating the pattern so you can create your anger and depression all by yourself.
C: I've never thought of it that way.
T: That is usually the problem, the way we think about things.

Conclusion

We might summarize the underlying philosophy of cognitive and cognitive-behavioural therapies in line with Descartes's 'I think, therefore I am'. People are often who they think they are, and behave the way they think they should behave. The cognitive approach to psychotherapy parallels the modern emphasis on the centrality of the mind. As an instrument for the client or patient to use, many of the techniques described in this chapter are relatively easy to grasp as they use the language of everyday thoughts, which can be interrupted and reframed where necessary through cognitive interventions on the part of the therapist, which are then taught to and caught by the client. As a form of therapy these techniques emphasize the client's control over that one part of them they apparently have more control over than anything else, their own thinking.

They may not be able to control events or other people, or even stop feelings bubbling to the surface; but they can, according to cognitive therapy, control their responses. As such it is easy to see why it has become an important adjunct to behavioural therapy, with the claims made for its effectiveness and speed of change being similar.

CHAPTER 6

Systems psychotherapy: couples, relationships and family psychotherapy

The systems approach to psychotherapy has developed both as a response, and in reaction, to the earlier schools of psychotherapy. Systems theory asks how the individual, who is the primary focus of other approaches to psychotherapy, can be understood without also being seen as a member of a couple and/or a family. The interventions and techniques of this approach therefore directly address the homeostasis of the relational and family system. Perhaps this is a natural evolution of psychotherapy, as it starts with the stress on insight into the past, then on learning behaviours, followed by an emphasis on feelings and then thinking. While other schools of psychotherapy define the causative factors as belonging to the family of origin, systems psychotherapies focus their attention directly on the family as a system of interdependent roles and rules. The primary task is to see how the relationships function. Within the context of a system, either all components or people within the system win, or they all lose. Systems theory considers relationships in the family as a single unity, making a win/lose competitive philosophy inapplicable.

The Structural Family Therapy school of Salvador Minuchin (Minuchin 1974, 1984, 1990, 1993; Minuchin and Fishman 1981) is concerned with the family structure, subsystems and boundaries. Minuchin's innovative contribution explores the interrelated family roles that the different members play and the psychological function that each serves to themselves and to the other family members. He believes that most symptoms are a by-product of the structural failings of the family system. For example, a family may not have enough boundaries, or the members are too disengaged due to the rigidity of the family system's boundaries. Interventions are designed to map out these structural weaknesses and plan direct remedies. Structural family therapy (Minuchin 1974) advocates paying attention to the family in formation and the family model, before attempting to use techniques to restructure the family. The goal is to get from 'Yes, but' to 'Yes, and' by boundary negotiation, broadening the focus through spreading the problem, relabelling, and restructuring tasks. Minuchin (Minuchin and Fishman 1981) stresses that techniques imply craftsmanship and attention to details. They are to be mastered, not just practiced. In their mastery, they lead to a therapeutic spontaneity.

An earlier contribution to systems theory was Gregory Bateson's (1980) concept of the double bind. The double bind presents an interpersonal situation in which a person receives contradictory messages and meets with disapproval no matter which way they respond. This is a no-win communication pattern. Bateson suggests that in an attempt to make sense of contradictory messages and avoid negative consequence, the family member can develop severe problems including schizophrenia – an idea given even greater credence by R.D. Laing in *The Divided Self* (1965). The client, caught between these two messages, is put into an impossibly stressful situation.

The Bowenian Family Therapy school of Murray Bowen (1978, 1985) aims to assist each member to identify their family relationship system, to become a better observer and control their own emotional reactions, to 'de-triangle' themselves from emotional situations. The goal is to develop a direct person-to-person relationship with as many family members as possible.

Whitaker's Experiential Family Therapy school (1953, 1981, 1988, 1989) stresses that a novice therapist's first task is to control their anxiety. Whitaker has stated that he personally always likes to get something out of the work for himself, so that therapy is a very personal experience for the psychotherapist as well as the family, making it a humanistic-existential encounter. The interventions aim to facilitate individual autonomy and a sense of belonging within the family. Whitaker sees each member of the family system as equally significant, tending to focus interventions on individual changes in order to change the whole. As a style, Whitaker's session sometimes appears undirected because he accepts and tracks all members' communications. As an existentialist, he does not accept responsibility for the direction and outcome of psychotherapy. The 'dance with the family' (Whitaker 1988) begins with the family, the family therapist joins, reframes and expands the communications (of which symptoms are a part) to challenge the rigidities and creates new pathways to grow. He warns that the secret to unhappiness is getting what you want.

The Humanistic Family Therapy school of Virginia Satir (1967, 1972, 1975, 1976, 1983a, b, 1991) develops a style of intervention that is personalized, experiential and extremely popular among professional clinicians working with family systems. Satir believes that all interventions should facilitate unique individual growth as positive self-esteem. They aim to facilitate a balance in emotional honesty and encourage direct communication patterns and rules among family members. The family need not remain isolated but can develop direct links to society. Satir (Bandler *et al.* 1976) states that there are three patterns of effective family therapy. The first is to assume that the family's coming for psychotherapy is a direct statement that they hope they can change. The second is that they recognize that they need assistance in making those changes. The third is that they accept the clinician as the guide to lead them in changing. Satir extends her categories of placater, blamer, computer and distracter to the family system interactions.

The Strategic Family Therapy school of Jay Haley (Haley 1971, 1976, 1984, 1985a, b; Haley and Hoffman 1967) and Cloe Madanes (1981) emphasizes strategic, goal-oriented interventions. Everything moves directly towards the alleviation of some specific dysfunction pattern within the family system. The therapist accepts responsibility for monitoring development and producing improvement. The strategic school sees the family system as a complex hierarchy of subsystems. The presenting symptom or problem is a statement of the family system, not the individual. The individual patient or client symptom or presenting problem serves the function of protecting the family in some way. A change in one part of the system will necessarily produce change in the system as a whole.

Madanes (1981) makes several distinctions in Strategic Family Therapy. She contrasts strategic interventions with a more traditional approach. She advocates interventions that focus on action over interpretation, on the presenting problem over generic growth, on a specific plan over a general method. She further advocates equality over professional hierarchy, on many meanings of language rather than one, and puts forward the advantages of being deliberately paradoxical or metaphorical instead of being trapped in straightforward communication. The essential element includes task directives that influence the unit, the power structure, the inter-personal influence and the family hierarchy.

The Solution Focused Family Therapy school (de Shazer 1982) uses the innovative hypnotherapy and psychotherapy of Milton H. Erickson as its foundation. It is representative of a brief intervention model. It is distinct in its emphasis on solutions and what is func-tional, instead of the usual focus on the problem. The focus is on what is changeable in the future rather than what is impossible and unchangeable about the past. Small changes initiate a ripple effect that can have significant long-range effects. The Brief Family Therapy model follows the pattern of pre-session planning, the prelude, data collecting, a consulting break for intervention designing and message giving.

In the headings that follow the different models of systems theory are drawn on as a background to the different aspects of couples and family therapy. By way of an extended illustration, a session is imag-ined in which the therapist (T) meets with a couple, Jack and Jill, showing how some of the techniques and interventions might be used in the various family and systems therapies.

Joining

Communication theory (Watzlawick *et al.* 1967) states that it is impossible not to communicate – all behaviours are communica-tion, and so not communicating is also a communication. Likewise, it is impossible not to have an effect. Simply by joining a family system the therapist will change that system. The question is whether the communication and effect of the therapist will be for the better or for the worse.

Often joining is more deliberate in the initial stages of psycho-therapy and decreases as the family accepts new interaction pat-terns. Joining is obviously an important aspect of any therapeutic interaction, where the therapist tries to establish contact and rap-port. The difficulty with joining in couples and family work is that a therapist must be able to join, disjoin and join again differently and with different people. The complexity of this task has led many therapists to use co-therapists, partly to help each other not to join to such an extent that they lose their 'therapeutic manoeuvrability' (Lyman Wynne 1986). Carl Whitaker (1988) uses a co-therapist to keep his countertransference problems within the 'stereoscopic vision' of the session. He advocates (1988: 57) that 'joining is the process of developing enough connection to at least feel that continuing is worth while'. The Milan School accepts that induction or joining into the family system is essential for therapists to be closely engaged. Co-therapist teams use a friendly but adversarial relationship with the family system.

Murray Bowen takes a middle position by joining the family system in the role as expert to whom all members direct their communications. Joining in this regard originates from a 'one-up' position. Joining may also occur by asking for information and clarification from the 'one-down' position. 'The successful introduction of a significant other person into an anxious or disturbed relationship system has the capacity to modify relationships within that system' (Bowen 1985: 342).

Minuchin and Fishman (1981) states that from the beginning, the family therapist must take some sort of leadership role. Most dysfunctional family members see themselves only as individuals rather than as members of a family system. They often see the 'identified patient' as the one with the problem rather than the symptom bearer for the entire family. The family therapist's task is to join the family as a system, as well as engage with each individual member. The family therapist then joins as a leader and expert, and as a member who will, while remaining calm, produce some resistance to the family homeostatic system. He or she may join the family in the close position by only confirming or recognizing the positives of all members. Alternatively, the family therapist may choose to join in the median position by being an active neutral listener and asking clarifying questions, or may join through a dis-engaged position of an expert and director of the therapeutic context. In joining (Minuchin and Fishman 1981) the family therapist earns the right to lead by his or her use of self in close, median and disengaged positions. The effectiveness of the therapy depends on the therapist's ability to join while challenging the family system.

The family is a social system with social roles. Conflict is a functional expression of growth and of changing adaptive needs. 'Conflict and the living process are one' (Ackerman 1961: 52). Within a family, conflict is a functional expression of competing representations of what the family is or ought to be, how it serves its members and how it fortifies its roles. Competition must be turned into co-operation because of a struggle for control. The therapist enters the family as an active participant or catalyst, stirring spontaneous interactions among the family members and with him or herself.

Ackerman (1967) writes that the therapist must join and get acquainted with the family by making personal contact with each member. The systems psychotherapist does rounds by addressing each by name and stating their age, by making clear that he has no previous history with the family, by eliciting background information and by offering encouragement.

The application of neurolinguistic programming to family psychotherapy (Bandler *et al.* 1976; Cameron-Bandler 1978) advocates the pattern of 'pacing' in order to join with a family system and establish rapport. One of the strongest patterns they advocate is the pacing or matching of the sensory representational systems of visual (seeing), auditory (hearing) or kinaesthetic (feeling).

The initial intervention which naturally follows, yet is imbedded in joining, is the family interview (Kempler 1974; Haley 1976). The interview starts as a family conversation. The healthier the family, the more easily they talk to each other. The conversation reviews the family pattern of interrelating and establishes the family as the major problem-solving unit, takes a family history, uncovers the longings, searches for personal needs and refines the messages in the family system.

Illustration

> *T:* Hello. I'm . . . I hope you did not have to wait too long.
> *Jack:* No, we've actually just got here.
> *T:* Good. You're Jack?
> *Jack:* Yes.
> *T:* Nice to meet you, Jack. And you're Jill?
> *Jill:* Yes.
> *T:* Nice to meet you, Jill. Have either of you been in psychotherapy before?
> *Jack:* No.
> *Jill:* Yes.
> *T:* OK, Jill, did you find that useful and helpful?
> *Jill:* Yes, very.
> *T:* What did you find useful?
> *Jill:* It was good to have somebody to listen to me. Someone to talk with.
> *T:* How can I be of most help today? What brings you in here?

Jill: The problem's communication. We just don't communicate.

Jack: (*looks away as if bored*)

T: It appears you do, but you don't like what's being communicated.

Focus

Minuchin and Fishman (1981) describe focusing as a process similar to photography, where in a large montage the photographer picks out a scene that best represents the overall view or theme and zooms in on it. The focus is on process as opposed to a focus on the content. The focus is on *how* the family does things, rather than *what* they do. In challenging the family structure, a clinician may first focus on an individual, a subsystem or the whole family system. The goal is to move from a focus on the individual towards a healthy contributing part of the whole, selecting a focus from the flood of data and developing a theme whilst being aware of the therapist's possible tunnel vision, collusion with avoidance or imposing their own beliefs about what is important. The therapist also focuses on strengths not on family deficits.

Ackerman (1967, 1970a, b) highlights and focuses on different aspects of the family system. Seating positions may indicate power play. The therapist comments on non-verbal cues, and contrasts differences:

Illustration

T: Jack, I noticed you looked away when Jill said you had communication problems, as if you were bored.

Jack: So?

T: Do you agree that you have some communication problems?

Jack: I guess so. I don't know.

T: You don't know, or do you not like what you do know?

Jack: I guess I do not like what I do know.

T: And what do you know?

Jack: I know that when she wants to talk it's always that something's wrong.

Jill: No, I don't! I don't think something's always wrong!

Jack: Yes, you do!
Jill: No, I do not!
Jack: You do!
Jill: I do not!

Intensity

Minuchin and Fishman (1981) describe the use of intensity. At times, the intensity of the family structure may make it impossible for the family therapist to get their point across because it is below the family's normal threshold of response. The family therapist may be handicapped since they must model courtesy and respect while trying to convey their message to a family that does not use courtesy or respect in their normal interactions. There are different ways a therapist may use intensity: repeating the message, or having a family member repeat their message; getting the entire family to repeat a typical interaction, then changing the timing or distance; resisting doing anything thereby not entering the dysfunctional family pattern.

Illustration

T: Well thank you both, for that demonstration of how you communicate. Does this ever work for you at home?
Jack: No.
T: Well, it probably will not work for you here either. Let us see if we can focus on what just happened, so we can learn from it. Say what you said again, please.
Jill: Well, I don't think that everything is wrong!
Jack: Not everything, just me!
Jill: There you go again. It's always about you.
Jack: Well it is. You seem so unhappy with me.
Jill: No, I do not!
Jack: Yes you do!
T: Thank you. That is what I wanted, to focus on the intensity of the 'do–do not' exchange. Do you do this 'do–do not' pattern often?
Jack: Yes!
Jill: No!
T: Thank you for the variation, but it is the same pattern.

Re-framing

Re-framing goes into the deeper structure, purpose and meaning of the system's rules. The family members interpret all communications within their given frame of reference. Re-framing shifts the frame of reference to assist members to find a different meaning. For example, parents may interpret their teenager acting up as a sign of rebellion as opposed to normal individuation from the family into their social world. Jackson (1968) describes techniques for framing of the therapy as a whole and setting-up standards and expectations of meaning and intent, focusing on changing stereotypical repetitiveness.

Minuchin and Fishman (1981) state that family therapy starts with the clash of two different frames of reality. If everyone agreed on the frame of reference or reality there would not be a problem. By definition, a dysfunctional family is working from conflictual frames of reference or reality. The conflict may be between two or more family members, or between the frames of the family and the frames of society. The family therapist starts with the family's frames and begins to expand or modify them. Another type of re-framing is re-structuring (Minuchin and Fishman 1981) in which the family therapist challenges how the family subsystems function. A valuable re-framing in systems psychotherapy is that the identified patient, client or symptom is not the real problem. The problem is the family interactional patterns. The clinician or family psychotherapist views the identified patient or client, instead of a negative, as a positive protector and carrier of the family's burden and secrets.

Another valuable re-frame is that there are no problems, rather there are solutions that are not working. Brief Family Therapy (de Shazer 1982) is an attempt to change the family's frame of reference into new rules or definitions and behaviours by changing their perception of the situation. Cloe Madanes (1981) says the first strategic task is to define the presenting problem in a solvable way.

Illustration

T: Do either of you have any ideas about this?
Jill: He just doesn't want to talk about anything!
Jack: She just wants to complain!

T: So you each think the other one is creating the problem?

Jack: She is. I am just trying to stay out of trouble!

Jill: He is just trying to avoid taking responsibility.

T: So how have you tried to solve this 'do–do not' communication problem?

Jack: I just try to avoid it.

Jill: He just tries to avoid everything. I tell him so.

T: So the way you are trying to solve the problem is by using the exact same communication pattern that created it? No wonder it doesn't work. You both think the other person is the problem. You both have a valid point. Perhaps the problem is not either of you individually, but the way you communicate together. You are showing a win-lose attack pattern. In family systems, either you both win or you both lose. Right now, the way you are both doing it, you both lose. Is that what you want, both of you to lose?

Jack: No.

Jill: No.

T: What specifically do you want from each other?

The prompt or 'tell them'

Kempler (1974) of the Gestalt-Experiential School of Systems Psychotherapy encourages people to talk directly to each other. All third party conversations are considered to be gossip and to be discouraged. The therapist asks the individual family members to state directly what they think, feel, or want in the form of an 'I' statement, diverting communications directed to the therapist about another family member back to the family.

Illustration

Jill: I just want him to listen to me, to talk with me.

T: Tell him that.

Jill: I want you to talk with me.

Jack: But she always just complains about me.

T: Tell her that.

Jack: You just complain at me. Why should I listen to you?

Go-between

In contrast to prompting family members to talk directly, in becoming a go-between (Zuk 1981, 1986) the therapist acts as a mediator between individuals within a family. Zuk sees a tendency in dysfunctional families to have no dyads, only triads: a family triad consists of two people in interaction to the exclusion of the third. The dyad may also form an alliance or coalitions against a third member. The go-between then often has to take the side of the excluded or targeted individual in order to balance the power in the family system.

Similarly, Bowen (1985) advocates remaining disengaged from the family's emotional process by avoiding the family structure and having each member talk to the therapist in a factual calm voice. Minuchin and Fishman (1981) sees the go-between role by definition unfair, unethical and placing personal demands on the therapist. The family therapist, as a go-between, aims at 'unbalancing' by developing an affiliation with family members, alternating affiliations, ignoring family members, or entering a coalition against family members.

Illustration

T: Perhaps I can help. Talk to me, Jack, What do you want?
Jack: I want her to stop complaining.
T: Complaining is what you do not want. What do you want from her instead of complaining?
Jack: I want her to be happy.
T: Hold that thought. You want her to be happy. Now Jill, what do you want?
Jill: I want him to not turn away or look bored.
T: Again that is what you do not want. What do you want instead of turning away and boredom?
Jill: I want him to listen to me.
T: Hold that thought, you want him to listen.

Circular questioning

One way of handling communication that combines aspects of the prompt and the go-between is circular questioning. All communications within a system form patterns of circularity (Watzlawick *et al.* 1967). Every response has an effect that is part of a chain in a cause-and-effect circular response pattern. The beginning or end is hard, if not impossible, to ascertain in any circular pattern, including a family system. Systems theory considers this an uninterrupted sequence of exchanges.

Often in psychotherapy, the client directs questions at the psychotherapist. This process can be an attempt to get the psychotherapist to take their side and build an alliance against the others. The implied message suggests that the couple or family system does not have the needed resources. This goes against a central systems theory belief. The therapist redirects or circulates back the client's question to the individual or to another member of the system.

Illustration

> *T:* OK. Jack, you want Jill to be happy? Jill, you want Jack to listen?
> *Jack:* Yes.
> *Jill:* Yes.
> *T:* Is what you are doing getting what you want from the other person?
> *Jack:* No.
> *Jill:* No.
> *T:* Then Jack, who would know what you can do to get what you want, for Jill to be happy?
> *Jack:* I guess Jill.
> *T:* Good guess. Jill, who would know what you can do to get what you want, for Jack to listen?
> *Jill:* I guess Jack.
> *T:* Another good guess. You two are getting good at this. So, ask each other what you can do.
> *Jack:* (*to Jill*) What can I do to make you happy?
> *Jill:* Listen to me. What can I do to get you to listen to me?
> *Jack:* Be more positive.

Boundary making

One of the major problems with dysfunctional families is the enmeshment of roles and a lack of individual boundaries. In boundary making the therapist directly challenges the roles and rules of a dysfunctional family in order to create more psychological distance between individual family members or between family subsystems. The family therapist may switch focus from one individual or subsystem by creating an entirely different, previously non-existent subsystem. Specific time and spatial distance may be used to create new healthier boundaries, as simply as asking members to change chairs and only talk for a prescribed amount of time. Often while in the process of boundary making, the existing boundaries will be unbalanced. The entrance of the family therapist as an expert itself challenges and unbalances the family power hierarchy.

Bowenian theory involves two main variables; the degree of anxiety and the degree of integration of self. The family therapist (Bowen 1985) thinks of the family as a system of relationships, emotional fields and breakdowns in communications. Interventions facilitate the boundaries, enabling the differentiation of self from family triangles, the nuclear family emotional system, the family projection process, the multiple generation transmission process and sibling positioning. Bowen advocates the therapist staying neutral in the family emotional field and using his or her knowledge of triangles to focus on the process between members. 'The overall goal is to help individual family members to rise up out of the emotional togetherness that binds them' (Bowen 1985: 371).

Structural moves that challenge the boundaries (Sherman and Freeman 1986) include tracking, supporting generational boundaries, allying with a subsystem, strategic alliances, ritual, reversals and complementary challenges of belonging. Boundaries are challenged (Minuchin and Fishman 1981) by psychological distance, creating subsystems, spatial manoeuvres and altering the duration of any interaction.

Illustration

T: So Jack, do you tend to avoid conflict?
Jack: I guess so.
T: Jill, do you tend to be negative?
Jill: I suppose I do.
T: Again, you two are getting good at this. You both probably came from families that taught you your part of this pattern. It probably did not work to bring them

much joy and love either. You both have been playing out the roles with no chance of ever succeeding. Let us see if we can step outside the families you came from and create the family you want to be in. Again, you are in this together, you both win, or you both lose. The choice is yours.

Challenging

Whitaker (1988) uses challenge to produce change. Challenge to the existing family structure and rules produces some resistance since it threatens the homeostatic order. The family therapist may challenge the symptom, the family structure, or the family reality, who the family identifies as the patient, what they identify as the problem, who is in control, or what they perceive as important events, the family's world-view, their symbols, truths, and power structures. Whitaker seldom challenges the actual content of a communication, but rather the meaning communications hold for the individual imparting it, the individual receiving it and the family system as a whole. He often challenges dyadic communication by asking a third member to comment. He offers his own perceptions or brings in a universal statement.

In Minuchin's work (Minuchin and Fishman 1981), there are three strategies in challenging. The clinician may challenge the symptom, the family structure or the family reality. In challenging the symptom the therapist enters from the position that the family is wrong and that the problem is not the identified patient or symptom. In challenging the family structure, the therapist as an outsider monitors the increase and decrease in the proximity between members and subsystems. In challenging the family reality, the therapist accepts the family's as well as the individuals' construction of their own unique experience of reality. Using cognitive constructs, paradoxical interventions and emphasizing strengths, the family develops a new way of looking at their interactions. To facilitate a sense of complementarity, or experiencing belonging, the family therapist challenges the problem by expanding it to the whole family. He or she may challenge the linear control, one member controlling another, and the punctuation of events.

In Gestalt Family Therapy (Kempler 1974) one of the most obvious challenges is the top-dog/under-dog dynamic that makes a family dynamic into a win-lose persecutor-victim interaction.

Ackerman's (1967) approach uses blunt confrontation to challenge all members by asking, 'do you want to talk?' He or she points out insincerity, challenges hostility, reinforces respect for adult authority, returns to issues, transposes conflict back to parents and continuously reasserts control. The therapist may interpret, press for disclosure, or be purposely blunt to point out evasiveness and encourage a deeper emotional honesty.

Neurolinguistic programming (Bandler *et al.* 1976; Cameron-Bandler 1978) advocates the direct challenging of mind reading and complex equivalence. Mind reading is speaking for another individual in the system (what the speaker thinks they think). Complex equivalence is equating one thing with another.

Illustration

> *T:*   Jack, let's challenge your part in this, your avoidance of conflict. What's going on inside you?
>
> *Jack:* I just don't like it.
>
> *T:*   As you say that, you look hurt.
>
> *Jack:* Well it hurts to think that your partner doesn't even like you.
>
> *T:*   So you believe that her negativity is about you, and that she doesn't even like you?
>
> *Jack:* Yes.
>
> *T:*   Want to check that out? Ask her if that is true.
>
> *Jack:* (*to Jill*) Is it?
>
> *Jill:* No, I love you.
>
> *T:*   Jack, do you believe she loves you?
>
> *Jack:* Could have fooled me.
>
> *T:*   Sounds like she did. Jill, what is going on inside you when you are negative and complaining?
>
> *Jill:* I just hurt. I feel so all alone. I feel that he is the one who does not like me.
>
> *T:*   Jack, is that true, that it's you who does not like her?
>
> *Jack:* No, I love her too.
>
> *T:*   So you both attack the other, Jill through active complaining, and Jack through passive-aggressive withdrawal, because you're both hurting? You both love each other. You both attack the other out of your own *hurt*. You both wonder why there is so much distance here. It seems obvious to me.

Enactment

Enactment involves asking and encouraging the members present in the session to act out a problem scenario, rather than just talk about it. This allows the psychotherapist to witness the actual communication interaction and to see all sides of the interaction. Clients often forget certain valuable pieces of information when talking about a situation. Enactment is more experiential and provides clues to forgotten factors. Enactment can also be used to help reframe a given situation or interaction, as a demonstration of normally occurring interactions. 'Enactment is the technique by which the therapist asks the family to dance in his presence' (Minuchin and Fishman 1981: 79).

Illustration

> *T:* I have an idea. Let's play it the way you would want it to be. Jack you start.
>
> *Jack:* Hi Jill, how are you? Tell me about your day.
>
> *Jill:* Hi, how was your day too?
>
> *Jack:* It was good. There wasn't much happening at work.
>
> *Jill:* Nothing new here either.
>
> *T:* You two are playing it safe. Enact a scene where you tell the other person about your hurt.
>
> *Jill:* When you don't listen, I think you don't love me.
>
> *Jack:* But I do love you. I don't listen because I don't want to hear about the negatives.
>
> *Jill:* I know.

An associated technique is family sculpting, pioneered by Virginia Satir (1972). When it is difficult for members of the system to communicate how they see the family system, they can be asked to position or arrange each person according to where they see them. The arrangements often surprise other family members and lead to greater awareness about why certain members feel and act the way they do. Satir extends her categories of placater, blamer, computer and distracter to family interactions incorporating them into the family sculpting interventions and techniques.

By contrast, Ackerman (1967) takes the initiative and rearranges the seats so that the parents can speak for themselves. He or she dares to have them demonstrate making roles explicit.

There are many variations of sociometric interventions and techniques in family therapy (Sherman and Freeman 1986). Sculpting is the most common. Others include the family choreography, the genogram, role card game, the ecomap or mapping the family network, family floor plans and family sociograms.

Illustration

T: I want you to stop and look at your posture and your position with each other. What do you see?

Jack: She's leaning forward.

Jill: He's leaning back.

T: I would like you both to exaggerate your positions right now. Jack, lean back further. Jill you lean further forward. If this were a sculpture, what would you call it?

Jack: The twin leaning towers of Pisa.

T: Are there any telephone lines between these two leaning towers?

Jill: No.

T: How do you feel leaning so far away from the other?

Jill: Lonely.

A special type of enactment is 'as if', described by Paul Watzlawick in Jeffrey Zeig's *What is Psychotherapy?* (1990). After obtaining a description of the problem, the therapist explores the solutions attempted that have not worked as yet, and then requests the client to act 'as if' the problem has been solved. Haley and Madanes, of the strategic school of intervention, may suggest that the family pretends that the world is different, a 'magic medicine pill' that, when swallowed, will change everything desired by the next morning. The therapist then finds out what those changes are and requests the family to act as if those changes had already occurred. Milton Erickson (Erickson and Rossi 1980: 205, 1989: 400) used to refer to this pseudo-orientation to time or future projection as the ability to look forward to the day that you could look back. Using future projection, he requests that they go forward in time to a point when they did not have the presenting problem, then look back and tell how they got there.

Illustration

T: Let's pretend that you both took a magic pill, one that would enable you to fix the problem over night. First, let

us enact the scene again, as if you were each the other
person. Jack, you sit where Jill is and lean in. Jill, you sit
where Jack is and lean away. How does it feel to be the
other person?

Jill: Well, as Jack, it really does look like she is coming after
me.

T: Jack?

Jack: I feel like Jack is running away.

T: OK. Now act as if you, as the other person, was sitting,
and responding the way you would want them to.

Jack: As Jill: 'I'm sorry I'm negative. I miss you and just want
you to let me know you care about me'.

Jill: *As Jack:* 'I do want to know about you. I love you too.
I know I turn away too much. I just hurt because I think
you are unhappy with me and your life with me'.

Jack: As Jill: 'I am happy with you and our life'.

Jill: *As Jack:* 'so am I'.

Jack: I will try to be more positive.

Jill: I will try to listen to everything positive or negative
if that is what you need to know I care.

T: Is that what you both really want to say to each other
anyway?

Jack/Jill: Yes.

T: Then say it. . . .

T: And if we sculpted that, what would it look like?
(*Jill and Jack hug each other.*)

Paradox and the double bind

Weeks (Zeig 1992) states that the goals of psychotherapy are all
paradoxical. The therapist must take control without appearing in
control. The therapist must maintain a positive view of the symptom as serving a purpose within the family system. They are the
opposite of what most clients see as the problem or expect from
their psychotherapist. Some paradoxical interventions and techniques (Sherman and Freeman 1986) include reframing, pretending
to have the symptoms, illusions of alternatives, prescribing indeci-
sion, joining the opposition and putting the client in control of the
symptom.

Minuchin and Fishman (1981) realize that the family system is
self-regulatory and that the symptom presented is a part of that

system. If the symptom disappears, it possibly exposes a far deeper problem. Therefore, the family therapist usually experiences resistance to direct attempts to alleviate a symptom. The family system is in contradiction, wanting to alleviate the problem symptom and wanting to hang on to its usefulness. The focus can shift from how to alleviate the problem, to what will happen if it is alleviated. Paradoxical interventions are best reserved for long-standing problems that have not responded to explanations, suggestions, interpretations and tasks. They require the family therapist to make an accurate assessment of the family's resistance, to have a firm conviction in the paradox and to follow it up.

A double bind is when two contradictory messages place the recipient in a no-win position, because each response will have negative consequences. A therapeutic double bind is a technique in which all responses offered receive an interpretation in a positive direction.

Illustration

T: Before we stop today or think we have accomplished something here, there are a few warnings I would like to give you. Please, go slow. Let us not change too fast. Change may produce or uncover some other problems the two of you are not ready to deal with yet.

Jack: That is what we came here for.

T: I understand that, and I hope you get some insight into yourself, the other person and your 'do-do not' pattern, that has never worked and never will. I just don't want you to get too hopeful and then feel disappointed.

Tasking or homework

Behavioural tasks (Sherman and Freeman 1986) include couples conferences, family councils, marriage contracts and caring days. Other tasks include positive exchanges, symbolism, gift giving, reading aloud and structured communication training.

The use of assignments as homework is not unique to family or systems psychotherapy. A task is a strategic intervention or technique designed specifically to promote change outside the psychotherapeutic context of the session. A task (Haley 1976, 1984) facilitates differences in behaviour, and subjective experience intensifies the relationship with the therapist and gathers information. Haley (1984) identifies different types of task or ordeal, including the straightforward task, the paradoxical ordeal and the therapist as an ordeal. An ordeal follows stages. The family therapist defines the problem clearly and the family must be committed to getting over the problem. The family therapist selects an ordeal and delivers the directive with a rationale. It must be precise and involve everyone. Directives (Haley 1976) have as their main goal people behaving differently and having a different subjective experience. The task directive must be reviewed and reported on whether done, not done, partially done or modified.

Madanes (1981) believes that strategic directives are the main therapeutic technique. There must be a plan in steps and stages. The goal of the planned intervention is to shift the family organization so the presenting problem is not necessary. Interventions take the form of directives about what to do inside and outside the interview.

Illustration

 T: It may be wise to develop a homework task you can practice until we meet again. You may decide not to do it at all or to modify it somewhat. Would you have any objection to practicing what we have learned today?
Jack/Jill: No.
 T: Good. The first task I have in mind is for you to purposely get into a 'do-do not' exchange. No content. Just one of you say 'do' and the other say 'do not.' I want you to get into it. Please feel free to push it to the extreme. OK?
Jack: OK.
Jill: Sounds like it may be fun.
 T: It wasn't when you did it earlier. The second task is for Jill to talk endlessly, only use negatives, and only talk about herself. Jack you just listen without any response or dialogue. OK?
Jack/Jill: OK.
 T: Then when she is done, Jack, I want you to run around the house like you are being chased. OK?
Jack: OK.
 T: I will ask you about these tasks the next time we meet.

Conclusions

Perhaps the most significant difference between individual and family therapy techniques is that it is the family that is the frame of reference. The therapist is active, and many of the techniques described above require the therapist to introduce ways of highlighting behaviours and assumptions. The family is seen as the problem-solving unit and resource, instead of the family unit being analysed as the source of problem formation, or in some instances totally ignored. Since the couple or the family are all involved this resource becomes available to the individual members seven days a week, not just during the session. Focus on the system, and on each of the members of it, means that family or systems therapy is less likely to feed into the narcissistic self-centredness that is the bane of individual psychotherapy. A healthier perspective is to see beyond the self into the connectedness of relationships, couples, families and communities.

Minuchin (1993) writes that the making of a family therapist and family healing includes looking at one's own family roots. The transition from individual to family therapist is a journey of transformation. But in conclusion, in a chapter which has of course concentrated on particular techniques, Minuchin and Fishman (1981) also remind us that it is important for a family therapist to develop beyond techniques.

C H A P T E R **7**

The growth of psychotherapeutic methods

Even as we write, the field of psychotherapy and counselling continues to grow and evolve. Further schools develop in response or reaction to those already in existence. Pioneers experiment with different ways of helping the client groups with which they work and some of these pioneers enable the birth of new movements. Some movements or schools are the result of other previously established movements or schools. Some have their roots in other cultures or traditions. Most have their own specific interventions and techniques, which, however much they differ from one another, work towards the same goal, the healing of the human condition.

Attention has already been drawn to the huge number of schools of psychotherapy and counselling that 'officially' exist. Having covered so much already, how do we choose what to select as we look at some other forms of therapy which appear to have achieved some standing. Inevitably our choice is personal, but we believe that the following are movements or schools of psychotherapy of which the well-informed therapist might like to be aware. Whether or not therapists choose to integrate these or earlier techniques that have been described is up to them, although the movement towards integrative work in the final chapter is examined. Even those therapists who stick to one set of techniques which have proven right for them should nevertheless be aware of what may have been the experience of some of their clients, referred from other therapists, or coming into therapy a second or third time from a different therapeutic background.

Neurolinguistic programming

John Grinder and Richard Bandler (Bandler and Grinder 1975, 1976, 1977, 1979, 1981, 1982) in developing neurolinguistic programming (NLP), studied leading communicators and psychotherapists to discover the patterns they used to help people. They paid close attention to such experts as Milton Erickson and Virginia Satir and gathered information on some specific patterns. One of these patterns was the use of representational systems. We each use our senses in order to 'make sense' of the world. Listen and you will hear people express the use of their senses in their language. They will say, they 'see' what you are saying. This suggests they are visualizing. It may 'sound' right to them, suggesting they are processing the information in an auditory sense. It may just 'feel' right, suggesting a kinaesthetic processing.

For example:

C: That does not sound like it makes sense to me.
T: How does it sound to you? How would it sound if it
did make sense? What would you hear that would make
sense?

In communication these 'predicates' can be 'paced' or matched to help establish rapport. The therapist can lead or 'overlap' them until communication takes place through all sense representational systems. The technique of pacing responds to the predicate of a statement such as 'I don't see it that way' with 'how do you see it?' An overlap technique might go on to ask: 'and as you see it that way, what do you tell yourself, and how does that make you feel?'

Neurolinguistic programming has developed a meta-model of linguistic patterns. The therapist listens for what NLP calls presupposition, cause and effect, mind reading, universal qualifiers, operators of necessity, lost performatives or referential indexes, unspecified verbs and nominalizations. These patterns are challenged by asking who? what? where? when? or how specifically? to develop a more complete model of the world.

NLP has developed a large number of further techniques, which will inevitably in this context mean little, but which can be found in NLP literature. These techniques include anchoring, anchoring collapse and sequencing, meta-programmes, strategies, eight-step reframing, change history, V/K dissociation, sub-modalities and swish patterns.

Illustration of anchor and collapse

> *T:* I would like you to think of the peace and calm you want, and anchor it by associating it in one hand.
>
> *C:* OK, I've got it.
>
> *T:* Now in the other hand I would like to place the context of where you would like to feel this peace and calm the most, and anchor it by associating it to that hand.
>
> *C:* OK.
>
> *T:* Now slowly and at your own pace bring your hands together and collapse the feeling of peace and calm into the context of where you want it the most.
>
> *C:* (*bringing hands together*) Wow!

Hypnosis and hypnotherapy

Milton H. Erickson, whose work influenced NLP, was also widely known and respected as a hypnotherapist (Zeig 1982; Haley 1985a, b). Hypnosis is of course a simple and time-honoured means to relax, and often used by people for weight control, smoking cessation, pain control and stress reduction. Rossi (Erickson and Rossi 1976, 1979, 1980, 1981, 1983, 1985, 1986; Rossi 1980), a respected authority on Ericksonian approaches to hypnosis and psychotherapy, cites three distinct characteristics of his approach. The first is the accessing and reviewing of the source of the problem. The second is a therapeutic reframing of the state-dependent problem with suggestions of correction. Third, the therapist gives the client suggestions for ongoing post-hypnotic self-healing.

While hypnotherapy uses different techniques, the process usually follows a very definite sequence. The sequence that follows is representative.

1 *Orientation to trance*: Before beginning hypnosis, a competent hypnotist educates the subject that a trance state is simply a relaxed, open or focused state of mind in which they are more suggestible. In that regard, the hypnotist must convince the subject of their good intent.

2 *Trance induction*: The hypnotist directs the subject to assume a relaxed body position and begins to offer instructions similar to the progressive relaxation described and used by the behaviourists.

This also begins to condition the subject to follow the hypnotist's instructions: often to hear only the hypnotherapist's voice and to block out other distractions.

3 *Suggestion (direct and indirect)*: Direct suggestion consists of a straight-forward verbal command to start doing some desired behaviour or stop doing some unwanted behaviour. Indirect suggestion is more open-ended, leaving more room for self-interpretation and discovery. Metaphors, story telling and guided imagery may also be used.

4 *Regression to the cause*: This is based on the idea that all unwanted problems are caused by earlier life experience. (This is a common idea of psychodynamic, humanistic and cognitive psychotherapy. It should be remembered that, of course, Freud started by using hypnosis before settling on his free association technique.) The therapist may direct the subject to go back in time to the cause of the current problem. The client reviews the source of the problem. At this point, the hypnotist might offer a new interpretation or perspective, or seek to provide a corrective experience.

5 *Post-hypnotic suggestion*: Post-hypnotic suggestions might consciously and unconsciously be carried out after the hypnotic experience and in some future defined context. The hypnotist gives suggestions for continued self-healing.

6 *Re-orientation*: Slowly the subject follows directions to begin to pay more attention to the sights, sounds and feelings of the present situation. As the subject reorients to the present context, they may discuss the insights gained through the hypnotic experience.

Strategic psychotherapies

A number of therapies come under the general heading of problem-solving therapies, where the focus is not on the causative factors of symptoms, but directly on finding solutions. Such therapies might variously be called, strategic, brief intervention, problem solving, and solution oriented or solution focused psychotherapy.

Contributors to strategic intervention include Gerald Weeks, Paul Watzlawick and Richard Fisch (Zeig 1992) of the Mental Research Institute in Palo Alto, California, USA (Watzlawick *et al.* 1967, 1974). Brief intervention has been developed by de Shazer (1982, 1985, 1988) and O'Hanlon (1987a, b, 1990, 1999).

One of the major ideas in strategic intervention is that the problem is not the problem. The problem is trying solutions that do not work. The focus on problem solving makes the primary focus of treatment what the client is doing to get 'unstuck'. De Shazer sees brief therapy as co-operative, more a meeting of the client's goals than a cure of illness, or 'fixing' a broken psyche. Strategic psychotherapy states that the map (the client's internal representation) is not the territory, but rather the external reality.

Lankton (1980, 1983, 1986, 1988, 1991) has applied many principles, learned from Milton H. Erickson, to strategic psychotherapy. He believes in a non-pathological model. The psychotherapist should actively use techniques that indirectly influence clients to change, thus leaving them with the feeling they have done it themselves and therefore empowering them. He also suggests that the therapist's interventions should pleasantly engage and enchant the client.

O'Hanlon (1999) sums it up well in saying 'change the do or change the view', but change something. If you always do what you have always done, you will always get what you always got. Popular advice says if it does not work try it harder. The strategic psychotherapist suggests doing something, or anything, else!

Some ways of intervening include:

1 *Exceptions*: Exceptions change the focus of psychotherapy from what causes a problem to what is the client doing when they do not have it. The therapist challenges the universal perception that the client is 'always' in this problem state. The exception focuses on a time when the client is not depressed, or less depressed, or how will they be when they are no longer depressed. This allows the therapist to begin to access a 'map' of solutions.
2 *Paradox*: A particular technique in strategic intervention is the use of paradoxical injunction. The use of reverse psychology is applied. The therapist asks the client to become more depressed or anxious.
3 *Tasking*: Often a particular task is associated or linked with the original problem, making it less possible to follow through. The task interrupts the problem pattern. Jay Haley (1990) refers to this as 'ordeal therapy' where the symptoms become such an ordeal that the client voluntarily gives them up. A therapist might therefore set as a task, for homework or in the session, paying attention to when the client is anxious and when he or she is not, so they can tell the difference. They are asked not to try and make the anxiety come or go away, just monitor it.

Alcoholics Anonymous 12-step self-help programme

Most people credit a man known as Bill W. (2000) for starting the 12-step movement in 1934, which is best known in connection with Alcoholics Anonymous (AA), although the 12-steps of recovery apply to many different conditions. In the addiction field, it has the highest rate of successful recovery. While the steps have a generic spiritual basis, they might be seen in applying also to other psychotherapeutic processes.

Step 1: We admit we are powerless over our addiction – that our lives have become unmanageable.
Step 2: Come to believe that a Power greater than ourselves can restore us to sanity.
Step 3: Make a decision to turn our will and our lives over to the care of God (as we understand the term).
Step 4: Make a searching and fearless moral inventory of ourselves: Any client needs to take a good healthy look at themselves.
Step 5: Admit to God, to ourselves and to another human being the exact nature of our wrongs.
Step 6: We are entirely ready to have God remove all these defects of character.
Step 7: Humbly ask God to remove our shortcomings.
Step 8: Make a list of all the people we have harmed and be willing to make amends to all of them.
Step 9: Make direct amends to such people, wherever possible, except when doing so would injure them or others.
Step 10: Continue to take personal inventory and when we are wrong promptly admit it.
Step 11: Seek through prayer and mediation to improve our relationship with God, praying only for knowledge of God's will for us and the power to carry that out.
Step 12: Having had a spiritual awakening as a result of these steps, we carry this message to others and practice these principles in all our affairs.

The 12-step movement usually takes the form of three modalities; group sharing, a 12-step study group and sponsorship. Group sharing is the basic meeting context for 12-step group. People get together and share their story. Members do not question or discuss. The purpose is simply to be open and honest. Many times the listeners can identify with the story and see themselves more objectively. The

12-step study group centres around sharing the topic of a specific step. This includes the actual writing out of the steps and, where possible, carrying them out. Sponsorship encourages finding someone else who can help direct the member along the steps. This is a mentor, teacher and parental type of relationship. Members are encouraged to call their sponsors on a regular basis, especially during times of crisis or problems.

Spiritual techniques

Although it is perhaps more accurate to place transpersonal psychotherapy within the humanistic-existential school, where it certainly draws upon the thinking of Jung and Maslow, transpersonal therapists suggest some techniques to alter consciousness. They view everyday consciousness and the ordinary sense of self as very limited and believe it is important to move towards transcending the normal sense of self and consciousness. In this respect the transpersonal school draws on both eastern and western spiritual disciplines (Wilber 1979, 1980), including the use of prayer, meditation and altered breathing.

Besides the incorporation of spiritual aspects into psychotherapy, one of the greatest contributions of the transpersonal school, is the reframing of problems and symptoms as a 'spiritual emergency' (Grof and Grof 1989). While the 12-step movement sees all addictions as based on 'spiritual bankruptcy', the transpersonal school of psychotherapy also sees current problems or symptoms as opportunities to go beyond normal states of personal consciousness in order to develop a higher perspective (Walsh and Vaughan 1993).

Shapiro (1987) notes that the process of transformation takes some very predictable steps, which parallel the usual stages encountered in traditional psychotherapy. The first step is some difficulty in breathing. The next is the wandering mind. Finally, the person begins to relax. This is usually followed by the development of a detached observation of the self. This is often where more traditional psychotherapies stop, staying with conscious cognitive and behavioural capacity. The transpersonal school steps beyond normal awareness into an altered state of higher consciousness, that is timeless and goal-less, having a holistic mode of perceiving without the usual evaluating or interpreting of ordinary mental processes. This state of awareness can deepen relationships with nature, with others, with oneself and can open the person to peak or mystical experiences.

Breathing

Yoga is one technique often used to alter consciousness. Various breathing exercises are utilized, from slow deep rhythmic breathing to fast paced panting or hyperventilation. In some modalities of the past (particularly in the hippie culture of the 1960s), in an effort to expand and alter consciousness, some schools experimented with the use of psychedelic drugs, although it was found that deep breathing could be used to similar effect.

Prayer

Prayer encourages the individual to converse with a higher level of consciousness – God, Ultimate Reality, etc. Those who have a strong religious or spiritual background can often use prayer to re-establish their spiritual connectedness or roots. Spiritual or religious counselling sometimes starts and ends in prayer, even though the main part of the session may use standard methods in line with whatever modality the counsellor practices.

Meditation

Most transpersonal therapists consider meditation the ultimate tool or path to higher consciousness. All schools of transpersonal thought teach meditation, through concentration or through emptying. Zen may be used as a transpersonal form of psychotherapy. Zen refers to a philosophical perspective originating in China (Chan) and migrating to Japan (Zen). To reach beyond thinking, Zen schools apply two primary methods, Zazen meditation and koan. Zazen meditation is 'just sitting' with the mind empty and unfocused. Zen koans are questions that are meditated on until the student realizes that the mind, with its logical constraints, cannot answer all the questions of life.

Body-oriented psychotherapies

Orgone or Reichian therapy

Wilhelm Reich (1961a, b), who developed orgone psychotherapy, is considered by many to be the father of modern body-oriented psychotherapies, where an important factor in therapy is concentration on the physical state and reactions of the client (Baker 1967; Boadella 1973; Reich 1973). As a colleague of Freud's, Reich believed the unconscious originated in the physical and the biological. But in developing his ideas, he lost favour with the psychoanalytic schools. Reich considered the body to be the storehouse of the unconscious and that oxygen was the life force or orgone energy.

Reich (Baker 1967) sees the body as divided in seven segments, such as the ocular around the eyes, or the oral around the mouth (see Chapter 3 in the companion volume in this series, *Character and Personality Types* by Totton and Jacobs (2001), for a fuller description of Reichian typology). Reich suggests that the repression of energy in these different areas corresponds with muscle tension and a blockage of energy. He calls this character armouring, a physiological defence mechanism.

Reichian psychotherapy uses relaxation with deep breathing or hyperventilation or charging. As the oxygen increases in the body, tense muscles go into spasm. The therapist employs direct massage techniques to release the tension. Memories that originally created the tension and are left unconscious in the muscle memory of the body can become conscious through cathartic discharge, and thereby available for more traditional psychotherapeutic interventions.

Bioenergetics

Alexander Lowen (1958, 1967, 1970, 1972, 1975) expands Reich's theory even further. He considers the body to be a mirror of the character, providing clues to emotional disorders. Lowen (1975) says that every emotional problem is reflected in a disturbance of breathing, a decrease or distortion of body mobility and is expressed in muscle tension. Bioenergetics uses the language of the body to heal the problems of the mind. Lowen charts a course towards emotional fulfilment through body awareness and the recovery of a positive mind–body relationship. The release of this tension dissolves the emotional blockage through bioenergetic exercises or postures. The goal of these techniques is to return the capacity for pleasure, spontaneity and creativity to the body and the individual's life.

Lowen (1977) has developed a series of postures and movement to stress body segments and facilitate release. The client maintains each posture or movement while breathing, allowing the vibrations of the stressed muscles to build or charge. The body's ability to relax and experience the stress leads to a cathartic release or discharge. One unique apparatus or tool is the bioenergetic stool that is about 1.5 metres high with a rolled up blanket on top adding an additional six inches. The stool is used to lean back against or back over, further facilitating an increase in vibrations. The goals of these exercises are to increase the vibratory state of the body, to ground the client in their bodies, to deepen respiration, sharpen self-awareness and enlarge self-expression.

Alexander technique

The Alexander Technique (Matthias 1984) is an entire system of body re-education through one singular technique. Correct posture lengthens the spine allowing more room for the neuron signals to go out into the body, allowing a greater responsiveness and ability to perform well in life. Alexander has students visualize a string pulling upwards tied to the top of their head. Posture is one of the behavioural clues used in diagnosis. It is believed that assuming the posture of depression or anxiety can help trigger or induce it, and that similarly assuming a straight posture can access states of heath and well-being.

Rolfing

Rolfing is the nickname given to structural integration as developed by Ida Rolf (1975), a form of deep body massage to bring the major segments of the body (head, shoulders, thorax, pelvis and legs) into vertical alignment (Pierce 1976). This alignment creates an efficient and graceful relationship between gravity and the body allowing it to return to a state of balance (Rolf 1962).

A course of treatment takes ten sessions, each focusing on a different body part or segment. The idea behind rolfing is to move the muscle fascia, the sheaf holding the muscle in place, and allow the body greater freedom of motion and flexibility (Johnson 1977). It is an attempt to realign the body to a vertical axis, and manipulate fasciae or connective tissue to allow the body to achieve a perfect upright symmetry. The ensuing pain is the sensation of freeing years of accumulated tension, which often brings about the cathartic release of stored repressed emotional conflict.

Awareness through movement

Feldenkrais (1949, 1972) has developed a style of psychotherapy based on becoming aware of how we move. By 'teaching' not 'treating', the client develops a better mind–body connection and a better relationship with the physical environment. Here again gravity is thought constantly to affect the stimulus received by the nervous system directly from muscular activity. Behaviour and muscular patterns are re-educated, integrating the physical and mental towards greater maturity.

Feldenkrais has designed a series of exercises, which the student does slowly and with full awareness, aimed at improving posture, vision, imagination, personal awareness, self-image and human potential. Practical lessons include good posture, action, movement, breathing, coordination of flexor and extensors, pelvic movement, the carriage of the head as it effects the musculature, self-image, spatial relationships, eye movements organizing body movement and the conscious helping the unconscious. An example of a simple exercise begins with the student standing upright with arms out to their side. They rotate or twist towards the back to determine their range of motion. They then do a series of slow movements in which the head moves in the opposite direction to the arms. When the student retests their range of motion they usually show a dramatic increase.

Meridian tapping or energy field therapies

Meridian tapping is a relatively new area in healing and psychotherapy. Meridians are the energy circuitry used by traditional Chinese medicine in acupuncture and acupressure. It is the blocking of the energy flowing through the meridians that creates ill health both physically and emotionally. Other forms of therapy branch out from these ideas.

Thought field therapy (TFT)

Thought field therapy is the exclusive creation of R.J. Callahan (1985, 1991). After many years of doing traditional psychotherapy, he began to explore applied kinaesiology or muscle testing. Every muscle corresponds to an acupuncture energy meridian. A blockage of the meridian produces a weakening of the muscle. Each meridian also has a corresponding internal organ and emotion. The thoughts or emotions create an energy field. By assessing muscle strength, a skilled clinician can assess emotional conflicts by perturbations in the energy field. The therapist taps on the meridian end in a specific sequence, pattern, or algorithm, restoring the corresponding muscle to strength and releasing the corresponding emotional conflict in the flow of energy. A unique contribution was Callahan's discovery of reversal points for stubborn emotional problems that resisted treatment due to a reversal of the energy polarities. The specific technique in TFT has the client first assess the level of distress on a scale of one to ten. The client then holds that thought consistently, whilst tapping the end of meridians in a specific algorithm. The client follows with several directional eye rolls while tapping a point on the back of the hand referred to as the gamut point. Another round of the tapping algorithm and finally the client reassesses the level of distress on the scale of one to ten. The clinician repeats the process until the assessment reaches zero.

Emotional freedom technique (EFT)

Craig and Fowlie (1995) have adapted emotional freedom technique (EFT) from the Callahan TFT. EFT has been reported as a universal healing aid like a psychological version of acupuncture to restore balance to the body's energy system by tapping, not puncturing, selected points along the energy meridians whilst focusing on the problem. The major difference is that in TFT there is a specific algorithm for a diagnosis, meaning the therapist has several possible treatment sequences. In EFT, the client is directed to tap on all the possible spots; therefore there is only one 'recipe' rather than many 'algorithms'.

Eye movement desensitization and reprocessing (EMDR)

Eye movements and positions are thought by some therapists to access different sensory representational systems and different hemispheres of the brain. Eye movements on the right side usually access the more creative left hemisphere of the brain while movements on the left side access the more logical and linear left hemisphere of the brain. Trauma may be stuck within one sensory representational system or brain hemisphere and, by rolling the eyes, the stored information becomes accessible to other resources for mental processing and resolution.

Francine Shapiro discovered eye movement desensitization and reprocessing whilst walking. She noted that thinking about certain subjects and rolling her eyes were incompatible. EMDR is presented as a time-efficient, comprehensive methodology (Shapiro 1995) for the treatment of disturbing experiences. EMDR follows an eight-phase treatment plan:

1 Taking the client history and the treatment planning for client readiness and safety.
2 Preparation, by establishing a clinical stance and explaining the theory.
3 Selecting a representative picture, identifying the negative cognition and developing a positive cognition.
4 Desensitization of the negative cognition and associative processing.
5 Installation of a positive cognition.
6 Scanning the body, assessing for any residual tension, tightness or unusual sensations.
7 Safety assessment, debriefing and closure.
8 Re-evaluation of the standard EMDR protocol and concluding psychotherapy.

One particular technique is to have the client focus on the representative picture and negative cognition whilst following the clinician's fingers with their eye movements. The utilization of EMDR has been extended (Mansfield 1998) to many innovative applications.

Psychopharmacology

For the sake of completeness, and obviously because some therapists are also medically qualified and able to prescribe drugs, this survey of other therapeutic methods is concluded with reference to a different form of intervention, psychopharmacology. Recent research supports the concept that chemical imbalances in the physical body create many emotional and mental problems or symptoms. Since the formation of the problem is therefore thought to be on a biological level, it is appropriate that the patient is prescribed a chemical/biological intervention. Research suggests that by introducing a chemical into the biological system it can stimulate the production of the needed chemical, or chemical intervention can be used to counteract a symptom by offering the opposite chemical reaction. Depressed clients may receive stimulants. Anxious clients may receive sedatives.

Only a qualified medical professional can make adequate medical diagnosis and prescribe controlled substances. Nevertheless it may be necessary for any psychotherapist to have some knowledge of the effects of chemical interventions, as well as the side effects as they may be experienced by the patient, or perceived by the therapist, when working with patients who are on medication (see Gitlin 1996; Stahl and Munter 2000; Julien 2001; Preston and Johnson 2001; Preston *et al.* 2001). It may also be necessary to refer patients to medical practitioners from time to time, to enable sufficient control of distressing states, which are otherwise obviating the effectiveness of psychotherapy.

Conclusion

With the development of new modalities there come new types of intervention. To those who are not familiar with many of the techniques described in this chapter, there may be greater scepticism than even exists in relation to the major branches of psychotherapy that are not one's own. Of course there are also a large number of people who believe in the effectiveness of the ideas described above. Studies of outcome are clearly necessary to determine which methods achieve what they claim, although that is not the purpose of this volume (see, rather, the companion volume by Syme and Elton Wilson, *Objectives and Outcomes*). Perhaps there are as many techniques as there are types of person. What is important is that for every person or problem a solution is found, and it is surely beyond question that the development of technique arises from dissatisfaction with the results of present interventions. That is the way it has been in psychotherapy since Freud abandoned the crude methods of nineteenth-century psychiatry, especially hypnosis. Others have followed his lead, discovering the value of word association, play therapy and other developments spawned in the twentieth century. It is not surprising that people think that for every problem, there must be a solution, and if the present solution does not work, another must be found.

CHAPTER 8

Contrast, integration and conclusions

Many types of intervention and technique employed in a variety of therapeutic schools have been discussed in the preceding chapters. Now the attention is shifted from description to a more personal view of the similarities and differences between the orientation of the major schools of psychotherapy. A short critique of the major schools is offered and the important question of how therapists might learn from each other by way of integrating their best knowledge of effective methods of working is considered.

Contrasting interventions and techniques

There are two ways of viewing the contrasts in interventions and techniques in psychotherapy. The first is to see how different interventions and techniques might lead to the same goal or outcome. The second is to see how the same (or similar) ways of working might in fact lead to different goals or objectives.

The first perspective is the easiest to explain and illustrate. It is generally accepted that psychotherapy has a single goal – the facilitation of change – although some psychoanalysts might maintain that it is less about promoting change and more about a research method for exploring the psyche. Nevertheless, most people see a therapist to achieve a positive outcome such as the removal of an unwanted symptom, the fulfilment of a goal, or the reaching of a life objective. The different ways of practicing psychotherapy have been developed specifically to effect these changes, new methods proliferating perhaps because of dissatisfaction with ways that appeared to be less effective. The psychodynamic school uses interventions, usually called interpretations, which are intended to facilitate insight, or to provide new perspectives on the patient's experience and perceptions in childhood and later, and through the therapeutic relationship to provide a corrective emotional experience. The behaviourist schools may also investigate precedents in behavioural patterns, but believe that change comes about more through a planned programme of intervention, which includes negative reinforcement of unwanted behaviours and the positive reinforcement of desired behaviours. The existentialist/humanistic schools seek to achieve change through the promotion of a therapeutic milieu in which the client can grow, and through fuller awareness and expression of feelings. The cognitive psychotherapist enables change through challenging irrational and unrealistic beliefs. The systems school of psychotherapy posits change within the context of a family or system and therefore seeks to enable the relational or family system to examine the dynamics of the whole, not just of the identified patient. These types of difference are fairly obvious. One might therefore look a little more closely at different facets of a therapeutic process, to see what similarities and differences there are across the major schools examined in previous chapters.

Contrasting the main stages and aspects of therapy

We start by recognizing that the use of both individual and group therapy is a common factor in many of the major orientations, even if beyond that there are many more differences in the conduct both of group and individual therapy. Psychodynamic, behavioural, humanistic and cognitive psychotherapies nevertheless tend to work with the individual. Even if group therapy has definite value in psychoanalytic practice, the training to practice as a group therapist is often quite separate, there being no clear transferable skills from individual to group practice, even if many of the concepts employed are the same. In many of the humanistic schools group therapy is more like individual therapy in the group context, than therapy of the group. Cognitive and behavioural therapy is rarely offered in groups, except where there is training in social skills. Psychodrama and family and systems therapy clearly use the dynamics of groups and offer far more than individual therapy in the context of the group: indeed in family therapy there is a necessary shift away from identifying any one person as 'in the hot seat', that is as the designated patient.

Some general differences between individual and group therapy, whatever the orientation, needs to be noted. It can be both more and less threatening for many clients than individual treatment. The social context provides some sense of 'being-in-the-world' and may make the progress made in the group relationships more adaptable to life and circumstances outside the group. The group context encourages and provides peer responses and support, enabling members to realize how much they have in common, and that their responses to what they find about themselves or others are not unique. Group members are encouraged to be 'therapists' to each other as well as to be open to the learning that comes from others in the group in addition to the group therapist. Groups may be particularly valuable for those who wish to enter therapy to develop themselves psychologically, or to give as well as receive help. On the other hand, 'joining' the group, sometimes described as the first phase of group therapy, may lead to higher levels of anxiety at the start, than the more private and obviously separated situation of individual therapy, and it may be more difficult to retain clients in group therapy in the early stages. If support from the group is wider, so is exposure of oneself to the group initially more difficult.

The therapist working one-to-one will in most schools be taking account of the wider family and social context, although it is easy to be pulled into concentrating on the inner world of the client (psychoanalysis) or the here-and-now of the session (humanistic), or on overt behaviours and individual cognitions where the message is to do one's own thing and not get anxious about having to please others (cognitive-behavioural). What one-to-one therapy may therefore do is to encourage the introspection of the client, even perhaps the isolation of the client, reinforced because the therapist is the only figure who appears to matter.

The influence of the therapist can be immense (for good or for ill), although the way in which the therapist sees her or his role clearly varies from school to school. The psychodynamic approach suggests that the therapist becomes, at least to some extent, a substitute parent or partner. Transference is a key concept, whether or not it is actively interpreted. The humanistic schools might stress that the therapist's role is rather to 'walk alongside', endorsing a close, warm, accepting relationship for the exploration, awareness and expression of feelings. There may be more encouragement for the therapist to reciprocate in the sharing through their expression of their congruence and through being genuine in their responses, something which is by and large much less stressed in other schools. Yet by definition, the role and position of the humanistic psychotherapist is also one of some authority, which may lead to some confusion. The cognitive and behavioural schools might be said to stress the educative role and to use their authority as 'teacher-psychologists' to impart new ways of behaving or thinking to their clients. Perhaps systems and family therapists could be said to do both: to educate members of the family or system to understand more about what is going on in their dynamic relationships, and at the same time responding more personally about their own feelings of being in the system (in the session) as a model of how to understand and how to relate.

Establishing contact and rapport

In classical analysis therapists present as a blank screen on to which the patient projects conscious and unconscious ways of relating. The analytic frame and empathic attunement within the transference and counter-transference relationship provide a stimulus for the client's association and projections, which are used to develop interpretations; nevertheless it is also important to establish and maintain rapport, what has sometimes been called the positive transference.

It is our impression that in cognitive-behavioural work the establishment of rapport is not given high priority. Perhaps it is the humanistic orientation which most stresses, for example through the core conditions in person-centred therapy, the basis for establishment of an authentic therapeutic encounter facilitated through empathy and unconditional positive regard and using reflective and affective listening.

Information gathering

History taking has always been important within the psychodynamic approach, although the way that this is done varies. Some analysts like to spend time before the start of the analysis proper in taking a full history, which involves actively asking more questions than would be the case in the analysis itself. Other psychodynamic therapists prefer to gather the history in the course of the therapy itself, although many ask more questions in the assessment session in order to clarify certain crucial information about the client's suitability. A major recent development has been the advancement of the concept of 'empathic attunement' in which the therapist becomes more immersed in the experience of the client, which itself provides a different type of information, enabling better detection of self-object failures; this helps development to recommence through the therapeutic relationship.

Behavioural therapists make thorough assessments, in order to delineate the extent of presenting issues and the triggers for unwanted behaviours, so that in turn they can draw up a detailed treatment plan. Cognitive therapists are similarly concerned with the sequence of various cognitions, as well as activating events and responses to them.

Humanistic therapists are particularly concerned with the here-and-now of the session and what the client wishes to tell them, rather than what the therapist wants to know. This may therefore mean that the client wishes to share considerable amounts of information, or very little, concentrating more on what they feel now than on what has happened to them. Some of the humanistic schools of psychotherapy use different approaches such as enactment, role-playing and psychodrama to bring experiences into the present, or to experience the present more fully, and to promote awareness rather than access factual information.

Systems therapy uses interviewing, challenging, questioning and enactment, including sculpting, to gather information.

The focus

Different therapeutic approaches measure change through insight, behaviour, integration, actualization, cognitions or balanced systems. The goal may also encompass changing the past, the present or the future. In order to achieve such goals and changes, interventions and techniques tend to focus on various aspects of the client.

Psychodynamic work focuses on the patient's insights, which appeals often to those with the wish to understand – sometimes called the epistomophilic drive. This usually concentrates on early development and relationships with primary caregivers. Campbell (1994) writes of 'erotic curiosity' where the patients' insights are reinforced through the therapist's attentive affirmations. While it is acknowledged that the past itself cannot be changed, interpretation of past experiences can shift, for instance from persecutory interpretations of parental behaviours to greater understanding of the complexity of parent–child relationships. We also note that in brief psychodynamic therapy considerable emphasis is placed on identifying a workable focus, around which most of the interpretations will be made.

Behavioural interventions focus on the unwanted behaviours and desired behaviours. Whilst the client cannot change the past, they can change in the present, learning to change future behaviours and responses by unlearning inappropriate responses and learning more appropriate responses. The cognitive psychotherapist accepts that certain beliefs have been learned in the past, but challenges them in the present so the client can have a better future. The focus is clearly on the patient's thought processes, and on replacing irrational beliefs with more rational and realistic ones that open up the possibility of a less anxious and more confident way of being.

Humanistic therapy focuses on full awareness and expression of affect or feelings, through a firm belief in the naturally occurring potential for growth and self-actualization. Different views are held on the significance of the past, from working with present feelings about past events, to dismissing the past as now of no importance.

Systems therapy focuses on the relational or family system, even though what is most obvious may be a particular problem in one member, with the goal of changing the system itself rather than the individual members.

Different forms of progressing the therapy

Free association in psychodynamic practice may appear to have something in common with the idea of the stream of consciousness in humanistic therapies, but the purpose is quite different. In psychodynamic therapy free association provides scope not just for the expression of everything that comes to mind, but also provides occasion for the therapist to hear slips of the tongue and other 'parapraxes', where the significance of the words, verbal play, double meanings, etc., are ways into possible unconscious thoughts. With the work of Kohut and those who have developed his concepts, the free flow of psychic material is harnessed to further the therapist's ability to perform the self-object function which is underdeveloped.

In the gestalt exercise, awareness continuum, the psychotherapist requests the client to express anything that comes into their awareness. In this and in other humanistic therapies the free expression is to allow feelings to come to the fore, to encourage awareness and expression of feeling. Catharsis may be a very important element in this process, enabling disowned or repressed emotions to find completion or closure, so too will the empathic response of the therapist be seen as both encouraging further expression, and supporting what has already been expressed. But catharsis has also always been a part of psychoanalysis, especially early in its development, when it was felt that unblocking repressed feelings could itself enable symptom cure.

In behavioural and cognitive therapies, however, there is nothing quite like this. Behaviourists may employ awareness techniques such as sitting and monitoring breathing as part of a relaxation-training programme; but this is quite a different type of experience that is being encouraged, with a totally different purpose, not so much to provoke material, but to set the mind more at rest. Detachment may be more important than immersing oneself in feelings or a verbal free-for-all. And this is a very different form of detachment to detachment from ego-functioning in transpersonal techniques such as breathing and meditation. Similarly cognitive techniques, in their focus on identifying and challenging irrational or unrealistic beliefs, prefer to bridge or track the internal cognitions in order to find the core irrational or unrealistic beliefs that limit the individual from achieving their desired goal. The focus here is on more exact identification of thinking, pinning it down rather than allowing it to wander anywhere.

Although free association may be encouraged, psychodynamic therapists are certain to prick up their ears when certain material seems to be emerging: childhood memories, sexual or aggressive fears or wishes, transference remarks, all might prove more of a resource for interpretations than current events. Similarly therapists of other schools may be more inclined to pick up certain material as being more in line with their interests: behavioural and cognitive therapists listening for signs of progress in achieving certain goals, or blocks that have prevented home tasks being carried through; and humanistic therapists are likely to home in on signs of feelings that could be more fully expressed. Systems therapists will be particularly alert to communications that reveal the dynamics of the family.

Dreams

Dream interpretation provides an excellent example of how the same content offered by the patient will be viewed differently by the various schools of psychotherapy, and also how the method of handling the dream will be different. For example, a woman coming into psychotherapy tells of a dream that she was cleaning her mother's house with a vacuum cleaner. How might each school handle the dream? (See also the companion volume in this series, *Words and Symbols* by Alred and Ellis.)

Classical psychoanalytic therapy might encourage the patient to explore the dream images further, to free associate to them, to see what underlying messages there may be to the obvious content. The focus of a Freudian interpretation might nonetheless be informed by dream symbolism with hints here of phallic content, perhaps oedipal conflicts, or penis envy. Her attempts at cleaning might be seen as clear signs of shame regarding these feelings. A Kleinian might wish to interpret along lines to do with the patient's feelings as a child towards her mother's body. More recent psychodynamic conceptions, such as those of Kohut (1984), might examine the themes of the dream in terms of the transference pole that is present in the therapy. A Jungian interpretation might be both analytical (concerned with the woman's relationship to her mother, or her care-taking persona) as well as interested in universal archetypes such as the mother goddess.

A behavioural or cognitive therapist is more likely to focus on the dream as expressing ordinary cognitions and behaviours. They would not necessarily deal with the dream at all unless the patient or client expressed some negative reactions and desired to condition the dream away. Or the dream interpretation may be limited to beliefs and behaviour that stem from the woman's thinking about having to clean to be loved; or it may be a useful illustration of possible perfectionist tendencies.

Some humanistic therapists might focus on dreams as representing disowned parts of the client. A gestalt psychotherapist might therefore have the client enact the dream by first being the woman, then the mother, and even being the vacuum cleaner, or the room receiving the cleaning. Such an approach might provide the woman with fuller awareness and expression of the content of her dream. Systems therapy would imply that the mother could also be part of the therapy, and the dream might be an opportunity to focus on the interrelationship between the different members of the family. The therapist might ask where the rest of the family is in the dream. Does the woman carry a 'cleaning' function for the family?

Active techniques

Psychodynamic therapy seldom uses active techniques whereby the therapist suggests a particular exercise. Nevertheless, the therapist may respond to the possibility of exploring certain feelings or relationships, by encouraging the patient to 'play' with an idea. So where a gestalt therapist might use an empty chair and ask the patient to address a significant person imagined to be sitting in the chair, a psychodynamic therapist might use a similar idea without altering the furniture in the room, or without setting up a deliberate piece of role-playing: 'What would you like to say to N. if he were here?'; 'What might his reply be?'

The stereotypical picture of the psychoanalytic therapist is of someone who is generally passive, sometimes even distant. Mears and Hobson (1977) have asserted that analysts must communicate warmth and empathy or else generate unnecessary anxiety in their patients.

Cognitive therapists tend not to use enactment, but behavioural therapists may use modelling, behavioural rehearsal or role-playing to practice new behavioural skills. Both are clearly much more direct in the way they work with the patient, asking questions to elicit detailed information on critical situations, developing treatment plans and following up homework tasks. Challenging and confrontation are also active techniques.

Humanistic therapists vary in how active they are in suggesting particular techniques that might be tried out, to further emotional awareness and expression. The humanistic therapist may use enactment, act fulfilment, or playing the part, as for example in the gestalt technique of 'be the . . .', where the therapist encourages clients to 'be' perhaps a disowned or repressed part of themselves or their experience, or to 'be' the opposite, or to develop empathy by 'being' the other people they meet. Psychodrama therapists are another example of a group that employs a very active technique, encouraging the client to develop a psychodrama enacting their conflict situation with other members on a stage. Some of these techniques are valuable in themselves, others as providing new material for the client to process in the ongoing therapy. On the other hand, humanistic therapists may actively engage in being as fully present as they can with the client, without actually suggesting any direction, or topic to be discussed: that, after all, is the essence of the person centred approach, that it is the client who takes the initiative.

Systems therapists often use enactment, such as the family sculpture that positions the members spatially to represent the family situation, which can then be followed by a sculpture of how the family might be if functioning more satisfactorily for all its members. They also adopt a passive role in watching carefully for the family interactions.

Outside the session

There is a further clear difference between some therapeutic approaches, where work outside the session is required as part of the therapy; and those where the therapist can assume that what develops in the session will be thought about during the intervening time between sessions, but not in any formalized way. It would be rare therefore for psychodynamic or humanistic therapists to set homework tasks, although they would assume that a naturally occurring generative process would help develop and integrate the actual psychotherapeutic process.

Behavioural and cognitive therapists, as well as systems therapists will use specific homework assignments, focusing on reinforcement of behaviours or the noting and challenging of commonly held beliefs, with homework tasks out of the session designed for each patient. Systems therapists also emphasize specific out-of-session homework assignments.

Defining success

Research on the different therapeutic approaches is referred to below, but here it should be stated that behavioural therapists have traditionally monitored progress, and the effectiveness of their methods, through measuring how far patients have been able to achieve clearly defined goals. Whilst research may have been important for the therapists in securing credibility for funding (for example), the idea of monitoring is also important for the patient, who is able to see success, and for this to reinforce the steps towards the desired goal. Cognitive therapists similarly define success as the elimination of those beliefs that stop the patients from achieving their stated desired goals, and work towards clear signs of change in cognitions.

On the other hand, traditionally, both psychodynamic and humanistic schools, perhaps for different reasons, have been generally slow to value research and, in any case, might claim that it is difficult to measure success. There have, of course, been exceptions – Rogers promoted research into person centred therapy, and Malan conducted research into brief analytic therapy, just to take two examples. It is often claimed in both schools that it is the process that matters, and that the pursuit of results is not the prime objective. Insight may be deepened, without necessarily inducing deep change, according to the analytic position; or becoming more integrated and actualized might also be seen as a goal in itself for the humanistic therapist, one that is difficult to measure.

Systems therapists might define success as a loving, open, nurturing system, where all members contribute to and individuate from the relational or family unit.

The emphasis on research in cognitive-behavioural therapy means that certain interventions are made after the end of therapy, including follow-up interviews or questionnaires. Follow-up is considered a necessity, to ascertain the success of treatment, although it might also serve the function of assisting the growth and advancement made during the treatment itself. This may therefore be a quite specific stage of therapy.

Other therapeutic schools often feel that follow-up, initiated by the therapist, either violates some ethical standards by intruding on patient privacy; or interferes with the ending of the therapy, which is a stage in itself that aims at closure. Some humanistic therapists, for example, would claim that when the therapeutic process is over, all the 'unfinished, disowned or incomplete business' is 'finished, owned or completed', and must be let go.

The ending

While behavioural and cognitive therapists have clearly defined goals that can be measured at the end of a clearly defined contract, and therefore are conscious of working towards a definite end, it is perhaps the psychoanalytic and psychodynamic school that places the greatest emphasis on working with the ending of the therapeutic relationship itself. This is true both of long-term and brief therapy, in the latter the ending being a major part of the agenda from the very beginning. In long-term therapy the ending phase is clearly defined once the agreement to end has been made, and may take considerable time. Of course, it is also true in extreme cases that it appears that psychoanalytic psychotherapy never ends!

The importance of working with the ending has been taken up by some of the humanistic-existentialist therapies as well, although it is our impression that interventions clearly addressing the ending are less common in humanistic therapy than in psychodynamic work.

A critique of psychotherapeutic interventions and techniques

It is evident that each school of therapy believes its methods are the most appropriate, even if some of them accept that their approach is not necessarily suited to every person. There has also been a tendency to be much more critical of other approaches as insufficient. It has already been observed how different techniques have developed because of dissatisfaction with existing methods of therapy. There is the danger of accepting stereotypical views of the different therapies, and reservations about some of the particular techniques that typify the major therapeutic orientations are given below.

For example, it has been suggested (e.g. Campbell 1994) that psychodynamic or psychoanalytic techniques concentrate too much on the patient's distorted unconscious intrapsychic conflicts and motivations, implying a rather negative view of the patient (indeed of humankind), and leading to the criticism that psychoanalytic interpretations can be rather persecutory. The psychoanalyst some-times appears to be in the position of one 'who knows everything' (Campbell 1994). Rejection by the patient of the therapist's inter-pretations are all too often viewed as resistance, which further rein-forces the assumption of the infallible expertise of the psychoanalyst. 'Heads I win, tails you lose' is a phrase which has sometimes been used to mock psychoanalytic interpretations, but there may be some truth in the jest. The authoritative style of the Freudian psycho-therapist may not be conducive to facilitating the development of autonomy (Ehrenberg and Ehrenberg 1986). It was noted in Chapter 2 how Lomas has criticized certain features of analysis, especially its emphasis on technique, because it allows therapists to hide behind interpretations and to protect themselves from any responsibility they may have for engendering resistance or failure in the treatment process. Concentration on the past risks ignoring the pressures of the present, and sometimes the perpetual quest for insight appears only to promote stagnation in terms of any change in the present. Classical psychoanalysis (four or five times weekly for many years) also pre-supposes patients willing and able to make a large commit-ment of time and money (Kovel 1976), with the result that tech-niques have not been generally developed, until recently, for quicker and less intensive work. Psychoanalytic and psychodynamic therapy is also best suited to those patients who already possess some level of verbal skills, have the ability to form attachments, have some genuine curiosity or introspection about themselves and can stand some level of frustration.

Behavioural therapy has its own limitations. It concentrates on observable change and measurable results, which may mean that its techniques are essentially limited to what can be shown to work. Whilst the advent of cognitive therapy has led to the broader focus of cognitive-behavioural therapy on behaviours, thought patterns and cognitive patterns alone may ignore the depth of feeling that is interfering with the client's normal functioning, and certainly would appear to other orientations to neglect aspects of the whole person. The techniques used in behavioural and cognitive therapy facilitate a type of tunnel vision that disregards, for example, the impact of the family system, whilst it views everything only as a stimulus to which the client is responding, making the form of interventions excessively narrow and restrictive. Behavioural and cognitive therapy is very directive and thus risks minimizing the responsibility of the client to explore their own dynamics and processes. Some would say that its methods can mask or avoid deeper problems (Kovel 1976). The interventions that emphasize 'it's all in your head' make 'changing your mind' easier said than done. The rational-emotive therapists, and perhaps cognitive-behavioural therapies generally, tend to be confrontational, although Transactional Analysis, which we have included because of its emphasis on understanding and changing scripts, has been described as less demanding of the client and interpersonally supportive (Ehrenberg and Ehrenberg 1986).

Humanistic therapy, according to Campbell (1994), has become an art form for the full awareness and expression of the human experience. Emotions, affect, or feelings become the language of that experience often minimizing or negating any other expression, such as what the client *thinks*. Expressive interventions and techniques tend to become overly dramatic, excessive ordeals, based on the inspirational zeal of the psychotherapist. The humanistic or client-centred psychotherapist (Rogers 1951) accepts responsibility only for providing a safe, accepting context or relationship for the client without accepting responsibility for the content or results of that relationship. The highly valued 'empathy' loses much of the professional objectivity needed to separate the client's needs and wants from those of the therapist. It is in humanistic psychotherapy that we are most likely to find the charismatic therapist, employing personal characteristics such as 'existential authenticity' and 'transparency of self', and following their 'intuition', 'gut' and 'spirit' towards growth and healing, so sometimes fostering a cult-like therapy and the image of the therapist as 'saviour' in the mind of the client. The warmth and acceptance of the therapeutic relationship may become a substitute for needs better met outside, within an equal and appropriate relationship. Unconditional positive regard for the person and the permissive atmosphere (Ehrenberg and Ehrenberg 1986) can easily confuse the client who may see them as acceptance and approval of the feeling the client is attempting to change (Kovel 1976). While some humanistic therapists emphasize that they are 'non-directive', the content and process they focus on in their empathic interventions can set a clear agenda for what the therapist appears to want to hear, and inevitably when responding the therapist does focus on one aspect rather than another and therefore 'unconsciously' moves the client in particular directions. While the person centred therapist uses positive affirmation and creates a positive environment, the gestalt psychotherapist is sometimes viewed as somewhat aggressive and arrogant, using intrusive confrontation and demands that can facilitate a feeling of victimization in the client (Ehrenberg and Ehrenberg 1986). Kovel (1976) suggests that gestalt techniques are less suited for the chronically psychotic client since they concentrate heavily on dealing with resistance and the expression of intense emotions. But it is also argued that the suspicion that some humanistic therapists have of assessment means that they may not take sufficient account of the difficulties working with very disturbed people.

Most psychotherapeutic approaches focus on the individual ego or identity. The system's approach is the only theoretical orientation that looks at how the individual fits with their family of origin or their current family context. Because of this difference, there is a need for very specialized training and supervision to prepare the psychotherapist for handling a multi-client encounter. Very few practicing therapists have adequate training, supervision or experience in this area, yet are doing marriage and family psychotherapy. In order to do systems psychotherapy it is necessary to get all parties to agree to attend. A task not easily arranged since by definition, the family system is dysfunctional. Too often, the participants do not see their own individual contribution to the family system dysfunction and enter blaming and telling stories to justify their position. Very few are willing, especially in the presence of others, to admit openly their own shortcomings. The systems theory itself supports and perpetuates a lack of personal responsibility in favour of a non-blaming environment of reacting. In defence of systems theory, it does further, or returns, the individual growth to the context of the family.

Can these different techniques be integrated?

The various methods of practising therapy assembled in this book are but a selection of the most commonly used techniques, without any comment being made on their relative efficacy. The problem with the structure of previous chapters is that it might suggest that therapists are single-minded and only draw on the methods they have learned in their training, their own experience of being in therapy and from their supervision (probably by a member of the same orientation). It is probably the case, however, that experienced therapists draw on much more than their own training. According to Corey (2001) the most frequently cited self-designation of therapists in surveys is the term 'eclectic'. This has a variety of meanings, which revolve around an approach to therapy that is based on matching the treatment to the client's characteristics and type of presenting problem. Since research (Bergin and Garfield 1994) has fairly well established that no single school or collection of techniques works for all clients and all presenting problems, this modern movement has emphasized the need for therapists to be able to use a variety of methods from different schools.

Such an approach is both wise and simplistic. It is true that therapists are well served by being familiar with a number of schools of therapy and their associated techniques. But the danger is in the indiscriminate use of techniques. This can arise in several ways. The therapist who practices as an eclectic may do so out of the therapist's own frustration with the progress of the therapy, rather than because using a different technique may benefit the client. So if therapy is 'stuck' this impasse must be examined in and of itself and not unblocked by applying some technique that will 'move the client along', as though the client is conceptualized as a log of wood. Some therapists, particularly less experienced ones, may approach therapy in an eclectic vein without due regard for the need to plan treatment and modify it as more data is revealed. This type of therapist uses many techniques in a somewhat random sequence, and so the therapy is more an occasion for a parade of techniques than a service to the needs and goals of the client.

A preferred term may be 'integrative therapist' rather than eclectic therapist, where different approaches have been truly integrated by the therapist before meeting the client, not in reaction to a difficult situation in therapy. But since by no means all 'eclectic therapists' use different techniques indiscriminately, the term 'integrative eclecticism' is as the guiding term for the combination of certain techniques and interventions that appear in this book or may be gleaned from other sources. The over-riding consideration is the effective use of interventions that are working in harmony to advance the client's goals. While this may be a basic theoretical position, it also suggests that the therapist is adaptable to each different client. This can only be done within a respectful consideration of the client's experience of therapy. The design and generation of a sequence of techniques should be focused on the ability of the client to benefit from the individual techniques as well as the impact of the sequence of techniques. Clients are not well served by chopping and changing from one school to another. They are the experiencing centre of the therapy. The impact of mismatched techniques is at least confusing to the client and in extreme situations may even damage clients and their ability to seek help.

Integrative eclecticism

Integrative eclecticism results from the blending of theoretical concepts and techniques into a harmonious personalized approach. Its promise is that of a unified system, empirically based and one that transcends narrow schools of therapy (see Corey 1991b: 426). It involves the *systematic integration* of both underlying principles and techniques. Norcross and Goldfried in their research (1992) identify three principles of eclecticism:

1 Pragmatic selection of whichever method best fits for a particular problem and/or client.
2 Combination of a couple of theories as the mainframe of a counsellor's practice.
3 Integration of a number of theories around the mainframe theories.

This theoretical mainframe is the foundation on which the therapist can then select and sequence techniques in order to assist this particular client dealing with the specified presenting problem.

The trend towards integrative eclecticism

Modern therapy training and research has increasingly recognized that there is no one universal theory of therapy. Some theories fit certain problems and/or clients but not others. The trend towards eclecticism and integration is important for the practice of therapy for two reasons:

1 Training must reflect the state of the profession's understanding, in that narrow approaches are not the most helpful.
2 Therapists need to focus on the client/problem interaction when selecting the way in which to proceed with therapy. Clients must be the determining factor, not a particular theory.

A framework for integrative eclecticism

Our discussion presents one proposal for the integrative selection and sequencing of techniques and interventions. This method attempts to make concrete the dimensions that will enable the therapist to combine techniques and interventions so as to minimize the chance of counter-productive combinations that may do more harm than good for the client. Six aspects of the process of therapy that are embodied in the techniques and interventions of the various schools are presented with a view to constructing a grid to analyse the treatment plan and in particular the sequence of techniques.

1 Goals

The first criterion is the level of the therapeutic goal aimed at by the technique or intervention. These goals range from the global to the specific and could include:

A personality reconstruction;
B uncovering the unconscious;
C finding meaning in life;
D learning adaptive behaviour patterns, e.g. in response to phobias;
E eradicating irrational beliefs, e.g. 'I'm a failure';
F expression of affect (feelings).

These goals exist on a continuum from specific/concrete to global and long term. The goals at each end of the continuum are not necessarily contradictory but in some sense variations of the general aim to assist clients in their life direction(s). As is clear to all schools of therapy, without clarification of goals, therapy is not likely to be helpful.

2 The therapist's role and function

The activity of the therapist and how this fits in with the goals is the next criteria. If the overall aim of therapy is to enable clients to recognize their strengths and the barriers that need to be changed for these strengths to be active in their life then the structure of therapy must reflect this in the stance and activity level of the therapist. The responsibility on the therapist is to always have implicit in his or her mind the question 'What effect am I having on this client in front of me at this time?': the level of directiveness is the central element here. Clients will need to be guided in their development of independence. Those techniques that utilize a very direct therapist involvement need to be designed to directly address autonomy issues. The measure of success is often stated as 'how is my work assisting my clients to move toward independence', which for the client might be expressed by the phrase, 'I feel I can go alone now!'

An issue that has arisen in recent times is that of cultural diversity. The interaction of therapist eclecticism and the culture of the client is very important as is the socioeconomic circumstances of the client.

3 The relationship between the client and the therapist

There is large agreement as to the importance of the relationship between the client and therapist. Some theories place a great deal of emphasis on the actual relationship (e.g. existential, person centred) whilst others do not regard the actual relationship as of central importance, even if they regard the relationship with the therapist in terms of transference as central. The role of the therapeutic relationship in the various techniques is often not explicit. Therapists indeed tend to create their own relationship style independently from their primary allegiance to particular schools. There are, however, techniques that do assume a level of therapeutic relationship that is more obviously connected than in other techniques (e.g. empathic attunement compared to Socratic debate).

4 Focus of the technique or intervention

All techniques and intervention are aimed at changing or highlighting something. A therapist would not use a technique if he or she was not wanting and expecting changes through the therapy to the betterment of the client. The three broad categories for change are affects (emotions), cognitions (thoughts) and behaviours (action patterns).

Criteria for considering combinations in techniques

The following six criteria are the result of both a literature review and some empirical findings. Each technique or intervention can be categorized as low, medium, or high on the six criteria. From this are generated two categories of three criteria (see Figure 8.1). A psychotherapist would only use a specific intervention or technique if they believed that it would facilitate the change requested by and for the betterment of the client. For example, if the therapist emphasized behaviours in a particular technique they would mark it high on the grid. If less emphasized, then medium and if used very little to never, then low. The two sets of criteria are grouped into two broad categories related to (1) the focus of therapy (affects, cognitions, behaviours) and (2) the therapist–client interaction

Technique or intervention	A	B	C	D	E	F

Rate each technique or intervention *H*igh, *M*edium, or *L*ow.
Key: A = affects; B = behaviours; C = cognitions; D = directiveness;
E = globality; F = importance of relationship.

Figure 8.1 Techniques and interventions evaluation grid.

(directiveness of the therapist, importance of the relationship in the theory, use of out-of-session activity).

The evaluation of these six criteria are by and large individual. Each therapist will be aware of their own emphasis in how they use each technique. There will probably be some agreement in broad terms on the differences between schools. For example behavioural techniques are very behaviourally specific, whereas humanistic techniques tend to be more global and focused on meaning and worth. Aside from these broad differences each therapist must determine how much they emphasize the therapeutic relationship, even (for example) whilst practicing out of a behavioural model.

Example of integrative eclecticism

A therapist is treating a client who presents with concerns about their intimate relationships. Treatment has begun using the psychodynamic technique of empathic attunement and interpretation of the transference as the therapist is of the gender of possible sexual interest to the client. The therapy does not proceed well even allowing for the role of resistance as postulated in psychodynamic theory. The therapist considers herself integrative and eclectic and so begins to explore what other techniques might be useful for this client.

The guidelines that have been presented in this chapter are then applied in the following manner:

1 List the techniques used to date.
2 Complete the six dimensions of the integration grid.
3 Write down the techniques that are under consideration.
4 Complete the integration grid for the proposed techniques.
5 Decide on those techniques that lie in adjacent locations to techniques already utilized.

The therapist in our example is considering using a couple of techniques to generate some relationship successes for her client, in order to increase motivation to look more closely at the deeper issues. The therapist is considering using assertiveness training and role-playing. This therapist tends to de-emphasize the relationship aspects for assertiveness training but to hold a more involved approach to role-playing. She now completes the integration grid as shown in Figure 8.2.

Technique or intervention	A	B	C	D	E	F
Empathic attunement	H	L	M	L	H	H
Interpretation of transference	H	L	H	M	M	H
Assertiveness training	M	H	L	H	L	L
Role-playing	M	M	M	M	L	M

Rate each technique or intervention *H*igh, *M*edium, or *L*ow.
Key: A = affects; B = behaviours; C = cognitions; D = directiveness;
E = globality; F = importance of relationship.

Figure 8.2 Worked example of a techniques and interventions evaluation grid.

In using the technique of empathic attunement, this therapist emphasized affects, globality and importance of the relationship. She pays some attention to cognitions but pays little attention to behaviours and being directive. Her classification of empathic attunement as she practiced it is thus HLMLHH. For the other three techniques that appear in the grid above, the same process applies.

Inspection of the grid soon reveals that the most appropriate technique for this client is role-playing. This is the case for several reasons. Firstly, the client's experience of the therapy will be more manageable if the client is not wrenched from one therapeutic emphasis to another. The prior techniques have created an expectation of therapy as supportive and largely paced by the client's revelations. The techniques that follow must not create a situation in which the client suddenly finds himself expected to proceed at a pace determined by the therapist's choice of task for the session. Both empathic attunement and interpretation of transference are more client paced than either assertiveness training or role-playing as practiced by this therapist. A client suddenly required to perform in a different mode may find the change more of a problem than the technique itself. Of the two proposed techniques the role-playing stays closer to the prior therapy experience (i.e. only one grade separation for affects, behaviours, directiveness and importance of the relationship), since the insights of the empathic attunement are potential data for the role-playing activities and the change in behavioural requirements is smaller than for assertiveness training (i.e. from L to M).

Conclusion

Philips (1992), in summarizing and evaluating the literature on psychotherapy, makes the following 12 points:

1 All psychotherapies produce approximately the same results.
2 Short-term psychotherapies are equal or better than long-term psychotherapies.
3 No individual psychotherapy shows a wide or decisive advantage over any other one.
4 Psychotherapies tend not to focus on society as a whole, but largely are geared towards young, attractive, verbal, intelligent and single types.
5 The psychotherapy attrition curve is negatively accelerating.
6 No individual client variable has shown acceptable validity for more than 10–20 per cent variance in outcome.
7 The generality of findings in psychotherapeutic outcome research has been on professional ratings not client ratings.
8 No hypothesis accounting for more than 10–20 per cent of outcome variance has been supported for relevant psychotherapy variables.
9 Short-term psychotherapy is not theory driven, as opposed to long-term psychotherapy, which is overloaded with empirically unsupported theories.
10 Psychotherapy outcome predictions, regardless of participants or variables, only account for 10–20 per cent of the variance.
11 Very little training emphasizes alternative schools of psychotherapy as opposed to the traditional in-depth models.
12 The delivery system as a contributor to psychotherapeutic effectiveness and efficiency has been all but neglected.

Research further suggests and supports the idea that despite the difference in theories, interventions and techniques, all psychotherapies are equally effective. Some researchers and critics suggest that psychotherapy is better accounted for as a placebo which gives people hope. Clients in a placebo control group demonstrate better improvement than a waiting list or no treatment group, but less improvement than those actually receiving treatment. Psychotherapy as a context, and the psychotherapist as a person, become the means of, or a promise for, support and hope for improvement.

Some researchers (Lambert 1989) suggest that the therapist relationship factor may account more for the success or failure of psychotherapy. Their research found that 70 per cent or more of successful subjects cited the personality of the psychotherapist as the most important causative factor. It was the psychotherapist as a person that helped them to understand the problem and encouraged them to face the problems. Simply the ability to talk to an understanding person leading to a greater self-understanding was very or extremely important.

Eysenck (1952) has studied and attacked the efficacy of psychotherapy. A statistic he quoted is still widely misused. Eysenck found that 67 per cent of patients got better without psychotherapy and that the same number (67 per cent) got better with it. What he did not cite (Bergin and Garfield 1978) was that the 67 per cent that got better without psychotherapy did so within two years, and the 67 per cent that got better with psychotherapy did so within two months.

What is clear from all this is that research has shown that the process of psychotherapy needs to be better understood, and that there is a place for the better understanding of the effectiveness of different interventions and techniques. There is also a need for better communication and shared information between researchers, psychotherapists and theoreticians for greater clarification of good therapeutic outcome and for more refinement in diagnostic categories for treatment planning. In addition there is a need to explore briefer time-limited forms of psychotherapy and to develop clearly defined interventions and techniques for specific problems. Finally there is a need for greater understanding of factors contributing to negative outcomes and effects. All this would considerably enhance the initial training and continuing professional development of psychotherapists and counsellors.

Two major factors contribute to the success of psychotherapy. The first is the courage of the client to be open and trusting enough to disclose their pains and fears, and to make the necessary changes in thought, feelings and behaviour in their lives. The second factor is the competence of the professional therapist. Furthermore, there are two aspects to the competence of the therapist: who the therapist is as a person and what the therapist does. Other volumes in this series look at efficacy (*Objectives and Outcomes*) and at the person of the therapist (*The Therapist's Use of Self*). This volume has been concerned with what the therapist does. Competence in the skills of delivering the different interventions and techniques described comes from good training, ongoing practice and careful supervision.

Psychotherapy is sometimes described as a science, sometimes as an art. We prefer to see it as both a craft and an art. The craft is developed through learning how to apply the specific interventions and techniques that have been the subject of this book. The art comes from a creative process inherent in each of us. Learn the craft well. But practice the art with humility and compassion.

References

Ackerman, N. (1961) *Exploring the Bases for Family Therapy*. New York, NY: Family Services Association of America.

Ackerman, N. (1967) *Expanding Theory and Practice in Family Therapy*. New York, NY: Family Service Association of America.

Ackerman, N. (1970a) *Family Process*. New York, NY: Basic Books.

Ackerman, N. (1970b) *Family Therapy in Transition*. Boston, MA: Little.

Adler, G. (1966) *Studies in Analytical Psychology*. London: Hodder and Stoughton.

Alvin, J. (1979) *Music Therapy for the Autistic Child*. New York, NY: Oxford University Press.

American Psychiatric Association (1994) *Diagnostic Criteria from DSM-IV*. Washington, DC: American Psychiatric Association.

Arkowitz, H. and Hannah, M.T. (1989) *Cognitive, behavior and psychodynamic therapies*, in A. Freeman, K. Simon, L.E. Beuter and H. Arkowitz (1989) *Comprehensive Handbook of Cognitive Therapy*. New York, NY: Plenum Press.

Atwood, G. and Stolorow, R. (1984) *Structures of Subjectivity: Explorations in Psychoanalytic Phenomenology*. Hillsdale, NJ: Analytic Press.

Axline, V. (1969) *Play Therapy*. New York, NY: Ballantine.

Baker, E.F. (1967) *Man In the Trap*. New York, NY: Discuss/Avon/Hearst Corp.

Bandler, R. and Grinder, J. (1975) *The Structure of Magic: Vol. 1*. Palo Alto, CA: Science and Behavior Books.

Bandler, R. and Grinder, J. (1976) *The Structure of Magic: Vol. 2*. Palo Alto, CA: Science and Behavior Books.

Bandler, R. and Grinder, J. (1977) *Patterns of the Hypnotic Techniques of Milton H. Erickson Vol. 1 & 2*. Cupertino, CA: Meta Publications.

Bandler, R. and Grinder, J. (1979) *Frogs Into Princes*. Moab, UT: Real People Press.

Bandler, R. and Grinder, J. (1981) *Trance-Formation*. Moab, UT: Real People Press.

Bandler, R. and Grinder, J. (1982) *Reframing*. Moab, UT: Real People Press.

Bandler, R., Grinder, J. and Satir, V. (1976) *Changing with Families*. Palo Alto, CA: Science and Behavior Books.

Bandura, A. (1969) *Principles of Behavior Modification*. New York, NY: Holt, Rinehart and Winston.

Barlow, D.H. and Rapee, R.M. (1997) *Mastering Stress*. Killara: Lifestyle Press.

Basch, M.F. (1988) *Understanding Psychotherapy*. New York, NY: Basic Books.

Basch, M.F. (1992) *Practicing Psychotherapy*. New York, NY: Basic Books.

Basch, M.F. (1995) *Doing Brief Psychotherapy*. New York, NY: Basic Books.

Bateson, G. (1980) *Step to an Ecology of Mind*. New York, NY: Ballantine.

Beck, A.T. and Emery, G. (1979) *Cognitive Therapy of Anxiety and Phobic Disorders*. Philadelphia, PA: Center for Cognitive Therapy.

Bergin, A.E. and Garfield, S.L. (1994) *Handbook of Psychotherapy and Behavior Change*, 4th edn. New York, NY: Wiley.

Berne, E. (1961) *Transactional Analysis in Psychotherapy*. New York, NY: Grove Press.

Berne, E. (1964) *Games People Play*. New York, NY: Grove Press.

Berne, E. (1972) *What Do You Say After You Say Hello: The Psychology of Human Destiny*. New York, NY: Grove Press.

Berne, E. (1976) *Beyond Games and Scripts*. New York, NY: Ballantine.

Berne, E. (1977) *Intuition and Ego States: The Origin of Transactional Analysis*. New York, NY: Harper & Row.

Bernstein, D.A. and Borkovic, T.D. (1973) *Progressive Relaxation Training*. Champaign, Ill: Research Press.

Bion, W.R. (1959) *Experiences in Groups*. New York, NY: Basic Books.

Boadella, D. (1973) *Wilhelm Reich: The Evolution of His Work*. New York, NY: Dell Publishing.

Bowen, M. (1978) *Family Therapy in Clinical Practice*. Northvale, NJ: Jason Aronson.

Bowen, M. (1985) *Family Therapy in Clinical Practice*, 2nd edn. New York, NY: Aronson.

Brown, T.A., O'Leary, T.A. and Barlow, D.H. (1993) Generalized anxiety disorder, in D.H. Barlow (ed.) *Clinical Handbook of Psychological Disorders*. New York, NY: Guilford Press, pp. 137–88.

Buber, M. (1974) *I-Thou*. New York, NY: MacMillian Publishing.

Callahan, R.J. (1985) *Five Minute Phobia Cure*. Wilmington, DE: Enterprise Publishing.

Callahan, R.J. (1991) *Why Do I Eat When I'm Not Hungry?* New York, NY: Avon Books.

Cameron-Bandler, L. (1978) *They Lived Happily Ever After*. Cupertino, CA: Meta Publications.

Campbell, T.W. (1994) *Beware the Talking Cure: Psychotherapy May Be Hazardous To Your Mental Health*. Boca Raton, FL: Upton Books.

Corey, G. (1991a) *A Case Approach to Counseling and Psychotherapy*. Pacific Grove, CA: Brooks/Cole Publishing Co.

Corey, G. (1991b) *Theory and Practice of Counseling and Psychotherapy*. Pacific Grove, CA: Brooks/Cole Publishing Co.

Corey, G. (2001) *Theory and Practice of Counseling and Psychotherapy*, 6th edn. Pacific Grove, CA: Brooks/Cole.

Craig, G. (1999) *EFT, An Introduction.* (video) Seal Ranch, CA.

Craig, G. and Fowlie, A. (1995) *Emotional Freedom Techniques, 6 Days at the Veterans Administration* (video). Seal Ranch, CA: EFT.

de Shazer, S. (1982) *Patterns of Brief Family Therapy.* New York, NY: Guilford Press.

de Shazer, S. (1985) *Keys to Solutions in Brief Therapy.* New York, NY: Norton.

de Shazer, S. (1988) *Clues: Investigating Solutions in Brief Therapy.* New York, NY: Norton.

Dupont, J. (ed.) (1985) *The Clinical Diary of Sandor Ferenczi.* New York, NY: Harvard University Press.

Dryden, W. and Golden, W. (1987) *Cognitive-Behavioral Approaches to Psychotherapy.* New York, NY: Hemisphere Publishing.

Ehrenberg, O. and Ehrenberg, M. (1986) *The Psychotherapy Maze: A Consumer's Guide to Getting In and Out of Therapy.* New York, NY: Fireside, Simon & Schuster.

Ellis, A. (1962) *Reason and Emotions in Psychotherapy.* Secaucus, NJ: Citadel Press.

Ellis, A. (1973) *Humanistic Psychotherapy: The Rational-Emotive Approach.* New York, NY: McGraw-Hill.

Ellis, A. (1985) *Overcoming Resistance: Rational-Emotive Therapy with Difficult Clients.* New York, NY: Springer.

Ellis, A. (1988) *How to Stubbornly Refuse to Make Yourself Miserable about Anything – Yes, Anything.* Secaucus, NJ: Lyle Stuart.

Ellis, A. and Dryden, W. (1987) *The Practice of Rational-Emotive Therapy.* New York, NY: Springer.

Ellis, A. and Grieger, R. (eds) (1986) *Handbook of Rational-Emotive Therapy.* New York, NY: Springer.

Ellis, A. and Harper, R.A. (1975) *A New Guide to Rational Living.* N. Hollywood, CA: Wilshire Books.

Engler, J. and Goleman, D. (1992) *The Consumer's Guide to Psychotherapy.* New York, NY: Fireside, Simon & Schuster.

Erickson, M.H. and Rossi, E.L. (1976) *Hypnotic Realities.* New York, NY: Irvington.

Erickson, M.H. and Rossi, E.L. (1979) *Hydrotherapy.* New York, NY: Irvington.

Erickson, M.H. and Rossi, E.L. (1980) *Collected Papers of Milton H. Erickson Volume 1, 2, 3, and 4.* New York, NY: Irvington.

Erickson, M.H. and Rossi, E.L. (1981) *Experiencing Hypnosis.* New York, NY: Irvington.

Erickson, M.H. and Rossi, E.L. (1985) *Life Reframing in Hypnosis.* New York, NY: Irvington.

Erickson, M.H. and Rossi, E.L. (1989) *Healing in Hypnosis.* New York, NY: Irvington.

Erickson, M.H. and Rossi, E.L. (1986) *Mind-Body Communication in Hypnotic Realities.* New York, NY: Irvington.

Espenak, L. (1981) *Dance Therapy: Theory and Application.* Springfield, Ill: Thomas.

Exiner, J. (1994) *Dance Therapy Redefined.* Springfield, Ill: Thomas.

Eysenck, H.J. (1952) The effects of psychotherapy, *Journal of Consulting Psychology*, 16: 319–24.

Feldenkrais, M. (1949) *Body and Mature Behavior.* New York, NY: International University Press.

Feldenkrais, M. (1972) *Awareness Though Movement.* New York, NY: Harper & Row.

Ferenczi, S. (1950) *Further Contributions to the Theory and Technique of Psychoanalysis.* London: The Hogarth Press.

Ferster, C.B., Nurnberger, J.I. and Levitt, E.B. (1962) The control of eating. *Journal of Mathetics*, 1: 87–109.

Flanders, S. (ed.) (1993) *The Dream Discourse Today.* London: Routledge.

Foreyt, J.P. and Rathjen, D.P. (1978) *Cognitive Behavior Therapy: Research and Application.* New York, NY: Plenum.

Foulkes, S.H. and Anthony, E.J. (1965) *Group Psychotherapy: the Psychoanalytic Approach*, 2nd edn. London: Penguin Books.

Frankl, V.E. (1946) *Man's Search for Meaning.* New York, NY: Washington Square Press/Pocket.

Frankl, V. (1968) *Psychotherapy and Existentialism.* New York, NY: Simon & Schuster.

Frankl, V.E. (1978) *The Unheard Cry for Meaning.* New York, NY: Simon & Schuster.

Frankl, V.E. (1980) *The Doctor and the Soul.* New York, NY: Random.

Frankl, V.E. (1988) *The Will to Meaning.* New York, NY: Meridan Books.

Frankl, V.E. (1997) *Man's Search for the Ultimate Meaning.* New York, NY: Perseus.

Freedheim, D.K. (1992) *The History of Psychotherapy: A Century of Change.* Washington, DC: American Psychological Association.

Freud, A. (1946) *The Psychoanalytical Treatment of Children.* New York, NY: International Universities Press.

Freud, A. (1966) *The Ego and Mechanisms of Defence* (revised edn). New York, NY: International Universities Press.

Freud, S. (1909/1955) Analysis of a Phobia in a five year old boy, in J. Strachey (ed.) *The Standard Edition of the Complete Works of Sigmund Freud*, vol 10. London: Hogarth Press.

Freud, S. (1912/1955) Recommendations to physicians practising psychoanalysis, in J. Strachey (ed.) *The Standard Edition of the Complete Works of Sigmund Freud*, vol 12. London: Hogarth Press.

Freud, S. (1913/1955) On beginning the treatment, in J. Strachey (ed.) *The Standard Edition of the Complete Works of Sigmund Freud*, vol 12. London: Hogarth Press.

Freud, S. (1921) *Group Psychology and the Analysis of the Ego.* Pelican Freud Library vol 12. London: Pelican.

Freud, S. and Breuer, J. (1895) *Studies on Hysteria*, vol 3. London: Pelican Freud Library.

Gardner, R.A. (1986) *Therapeutic Communication with Children: The Mutual Storytelling Technique in Child Psychotherapy*. New York, NY: Jason Aronson.

Gitlin, M.J. (1996) *The Psychotherapist's Guide to Psychopharmacology*. New York, NY: Simon & Schuster.

Glasser, W. (1965) *Reality Therapy*. New York, NY: Harper & Row.

Glasser, W. (1976) *Positive Addiction*. New York, NY: Harper & Row.

Glasser, W. (1989a) *Choice Theory, A New Psychology of Personal Freedom*. New York, NY: Harper Perennial.

Glasser, W. (1989b) *Control Theory in the Practice of Reality Therapy*. New York, NY: Harper & Row.

Goldiamond, I. (1965) Self-control procedures in personal behavior problems, *Psychological Reports*, 17: 851–68.

Granvold, D.K. (1994) *Cognitive and Behavioral Treatment*. Pacific Grove, CA: Brooks/Cole.

Greenson, R. (1967) *The Technique and Practice of Psycho-analysis*, vol 1. London: Hogarth Press.

Grof, S. and Grof, C. (eds) (1989) *Spiritual Emergency*. Los Angeles, CA: J.P. Tarcher.

Haley, J. (1971) *Changing Families: A Family Therapy Readers*. New York, NY: Grune & Stratton.

Haley, J. (1976) *Problem Solving Therapy*. San Francisco, CA: Jossey.

Haley, J. (1984) *Ordeal Therapy*. San Francisco, CA: Jossey Bass.

Haley, J. (1985a) *Conversations with Milton H. Erickson: Vol. 2 Changing Couple*. New York, NY: Triangle/Norton.

Haley, J. (1985b) *Conversations with Milton H. Erickson, Vol. 3 Changing Children and Families*. New York, NY: Triangle/Norton.

Haley, J. (1990) *Strategies of Psychotherapy*. New York, NY: Triangle Press.

Haley, J. and Hoffman, L. (1967) *Techniques of Family Therapy*. New York, NY: Basic Book.

Hargreaves, D.J. (1986) *Developmental Psychology of Music*. New York, NY: Cambridge University.

Hawton, K., Salkovskis, P., Kirk, J. and Clark, D. (1989) *Cognitive Behaviour Therapy for Psychiatric Problems: A Practical Guide*. New York, NY: Oxford University Press.

Hodges, D.A. (1996) *Handbook of Music Psychology*. San Antonio, TX: IMR.

Jackson, D. (1968) *Therapy, Communication, and Change*. Palo Alto, CA: Science and Behavior Books.

James, D. (1969) *Play Therapy: An Overview*. Oceanside, NY: Dabor.

Janov, A. (1970) *Primal Scream*. New York, NY: Pergigee.

Janov, A. (1972) *The Primal Revolutions*. New York, NY: Simon & Schuster.

Janov, A. (1980) *Prisoner of Pain*. Garden City, NY: Anchor Doubleday.

Janov, A. (1991) *The New Primal Scream*. Wilmington, DE: Enterprise.

Janov, A. (1996) *Why People Get Sick & How To Get Well*. W. Hollywood, CA: Dove.

Johnson, D. (1977) *The Protean Body*. New York, NY: Harper & Row.

Julien, R.M. (2001) *A Primer of Drug Action*. New York, NY: W.H. Freeman.

Jung, C.G. (1982) *The Collected Works of C.G. Jung, Vol. 2: Experimental Research*. New York, NY: Princeton University Press.

Kaplan, H.I., Sadock, B.J. and Grebb, J.A. (1994) *Synopsis of Psychiatry*, seventh edn. Baltimore, MD: Williams & Wilkins.

Kempler, W. (1974) *Principles of Gestalt Family Therapy*. Salt Lake City, UT: Desert Press.

Kendall, P.C. and Hollan, S.D. (1979) *Cognitive-Behavioral Interventions: Theory, Research, and Procedure*. New York, NY: Academic Press.

Kendall, P.C. and Hollan, S.D. (1981) *Assessment Strategies for Cognitive-Behavioral Interventions*. New York, NY: Academic Press.

King, L. (1999) *Committed Uncertainty in Psychotherapy: Essays in Honour of Peter Lomas*. London: Whurr Publishers.

Klein, M. (1932) *The Psychoanalysis of Children*. London: Hogarth Press.

Kohut, H. (1971) *The Analysis of the Self*. New York, NY: International Universities Press.

Kohut, H. (1977) *The Restoration of the Self*. New York, NY: International Universities Press.

Kohut, H. (1984) *How Does Analysis Cure*. Chicago, IL: University of Chicago Press.

Kovel, J. (1976) *A Complete Guide to Therapy: from Psychoanalysis to Behavior Modification*. New York, NY: Pantheon Books.

Laing, R.D. (1965) *The Divided Self*. New York, NY: Penguin Books.

Lambert, M.J. (1989) The individual therapist's contribution to psychotherapy process and outcome, *Clinical Psychology Review*, 9: 469–85.

Langs, R. (1982) *Psychotherapy: A Basic Text*. New York, NY: Aronson.

Lankton, S.R. (1980) *Practical Magic*. Cupertino, CA: Meta-Publications.

Lankton, S.R. (1983) *The Answer Within*. New York, NY: Brunner/Mazel.

Lankton, S.R. (1986) *Enchantment and Intervention*. New York, NY: Brunner/Mazel.

Lankton, S.R. (1988) *Developing Ericksonian Therapy*. New York, NY: Brunner/Mazel.

Lankton, S.R. (1991) *Tales of Enchantment*. New York, NY: Brunner/Mazel.

Lazarus, A.A. (1967) In support of technical eclecticism, *Psychological Reports*, 21: 415–16.

Lazarus, A.A. (1971) *Behavior Therapy and Beyond*. New York, NY: McGraw-Hill.

Lazarus, A.A. (1976) *Multimodal Behavior Therapy*. New York, NY: Springer.

Lazarus, A.A. (1981) *The Practice of Multimodal Therapy*. New York, NY: McGraw-Hill.

Lazarus, A. (1985) *Casebook of Multimodal Therapy*. New York, NY: Ivy Books.

Levy, F. (1988) *Dance/Movement Therapy*. Reston, NY: American Alliance for Dance.

Lichtenberg, J.D. (1989) *Psychoanalysis and Motivation*. Hillsdale, NJ: Analytic Press.

Lichtenberg, J.D., Lachmann, F.M. and Fosshage, J.L. (1996) *The Clinical Exchange*. Hillsdale, NJ: Analytic Press.

Loewenstein, R.M. (1982) *Practice and Precepts in Psychoanalytic Technique: Selected Papers of Rudolph M. Loewenstein.* New Haven, CT: Yale University Press.

Lomas, J. (1985) *First and Foremost in Community Health Centres.* Toronto, ON: University of Toronto Press.

Lomas, P. (1987) *The Limits of Interpretation.* London: Pelican Books.

Lowen, A. (1958) *The Language of the Body.* New York, NY: Grune & Stratton.

Lowen, A. (1967) *The Betrayal of the Body.* New York, NY: Grune & Stratton.

Lowen, A. (1970) *Pleasure.* New York, NY: Penguin Books.

Lowen, A. (1972) *Depression and the Body.* Baltimore, MD: Pelican.

Lowen, A. (1975) *Bioenergetics.* New York, NY: Penguin Books.

Lowen, A. (1977) *The Way to Vibrant Health.* New York, NY: Harper & Row.

Madanes, C. (1981) *Strategic Family Therapy.* San Francisco, CA: Jossey.

Mahoney, M.J. and Freeman, A. (1985) *Cognition and Psychotherapy.* New York, NY: Plenum.

Mansfield, P. (1998) *Extending EMDR.* New York, NY: Norton.

Maslow, A.H. (1968) *Towards a Psychology of Being.* Princeton, NJ: Van.

Maslow, A.H. (1970) *Motivation and Personality.* New York, NY: Harper & Row.

Matthias, A.F. (1984) *The Use of the Self.* Long Beach, CA: Centreline Press.

May, R. (1961) *Existential Psychology.* New York, NY: Random.

May, R. (1977) *The Meaning of Anxiety.* New York, NY: Norton.

May, R. (1983) *The Discovery of Being.* New York, NY: Norton.

May, R. (1989) *The Art of Counseling.* New York, NY: Gardner Press.

Mears, R. and Hobson, R. (1977) The persecutory therapist, *British Journal of Medical Psychology,* 50: 349–59.

Meichenbaum, D.H. (1977) *Cognitive-Behavior Modification.* New York, NY: Plenum.

Meissner, W. (1991) *What is Effective in Psychoanalytic Therapy.* New York, NY: Aronson.

Meyers, L. (1961) *Emotions and Meaning in Music.* Chicago, IL: University of Chicago.

Mischel, W. (1968) *Personality and Assessment.* New York, NY: Wiley.

Minuchin, S. (1974) *Families and Family Therapy.* Cambridge, MA: Harvard University.

Minuchin, S. (1984) *Family Kaleidoscope.* Cambridge, MA: Harvard University.

Minuchin, S. (1990) *Family Therapy Techniques.* New York, NY: Harvard University Press.

Minuchin, S. (1993) *Family Healing.* New York, NY: Free Press.

Minuchin, S. and Fishman, H.C. (1981) *Family Therapy Techniques.* Cambridge, MA: Harvard University.

Moreno, J.L. (1946) *Psychodrama Volume 1.* Beacon, NY: Beacon House.

Moreno, J.L. (1959) *Psychodrama Volume 2.* Beacon, NY: Beacon House.

Moreno, J.L. (1975) *Psychodrama Volume 3.* Beacon, NY: Beacon House.

Mursell, J.L. (1971) *Psychology of Music.* Westport, CN: Greenwood.

Naranjo, C. (1973) *The Techniques of Gestalt Therapy.* Berkeley, CA: The SAT Press.

Norcross, J.C. and Goldfried, M.R. (1992) *Handbook of Psychotherapy Integration.* New York, NY: Basic Books.

Oaklander, V. (1978) *Windows to Our Children.* Moab, UT: Real People Press.

O'Connor, K. (1997) *Play Therapy: Theory and Practice.* New York, NY: Wiley.

O'Hanlon, B. (1987a) *Shifting Context.* New York, NY: Guilford Press.

O'Hanlon, B. (1987b) *Taproots.* New York, NY: W.W. Norton.

O'Hanlon, B. (1990) *In Search of Solutions.* New York, NY: Norton.

O'Hanlon, B. (1999) *Do One Thing Different.* New York, NY: William.

Paolino, T.J. (1981) *Psychoanalytic Psychotherapy: Theory, Technique, Therapeutic Relationship and Treatability.* New York, NY: Brunner/Mazel.

Perls, F.S. (1947) *Ego, Hunger, and Aggression.* London: Allen & Unwin.

Perls, F.S. (1969) *Gestalt Therapy Verbatim.* Moab, UT: Real People Press.

Perls, F.S. (1973) *The Gestalt Approach and Eyewitness to Therapy.* New York, NY: Science & Behavioral Books.

Perls, F.S. (1975) *Gestalt Is.* Moab, UT: Real People Press.

Perls, F.S., Hefferline, R.F. and Goodman, P. (1951) *Gestalt Therapy.* New York, NY: Julian Press.

Pettijohn, T. (1986) *The Encyclopedic Dictionary of Psychology*, 3rd edn. Dushkin, CN: Guilford Press.

Philips, C. (1992) In J. Zeig (ed.) *The Evolution of Psychotherapy: The Second Conference.* New York, NY: Brunner/Mazel.

Pierce, R. (1976) *The Rolfing Technique.* Boulder, CO: Rolf Institute.

Pines, M. (ed.) (1985) *Bion and Group Psychotherapy.* London: Routledge, Kegan & Paul.

Polster, E. and Polster, M. (1973) *Gestalt Therapy Integrated.* New York, NY: Bruner/Mazel.

Preston, J.D. and Johnson, J. (2001) *Clinical Psychopharmacology Made Ridiculously Simple.* Miami, FL: MedMaster Publishing Group.

Preston, J.D., O'Neal, J.H. and Talaga, M.C. (2001) *Handbook of Clinical Psychopharmacology for Therapists.* Oakland, CA: New Harbinger Publications.

Pulver, S.E. (1995) The technique of psychoanalysis proper, in B.M. Moore and B.D. Fine (eds) *Psychoanalysis. The Major Concepts.* London: Yale University Press, pp. 5–25.

Reich, P. (1973) *The Book of Dreams.* Greenwich, CN: Fawcett Premier.

Reich, W. (1961a) *Character Analysis.* New York, NY: Pocket Books.

Reich, W. (1961b) *The Function of the Orgasm.* New York, NY: Pocket Books.

Rogers, C. (1951) *Client-Centered Therapy.* Boston, MA: Houghton Mifflin.

Rogers, C. (1961) *On Becoming a Person.* Boston, MA: Houghton Mifflin.

Rogers, C. (1977) *Carl Rogers on Personal Power.* New York, NY: Delacorte Press.

Rogers, C. (1980) *A Way of Being.* Boston, MA: Houghton Mifflin.

Rolf, I. (1962) *Rolfing.* Santa Monica, CA: Dennis-Landman.

Rolf, I. (1975) *What in the World is Rolfing?* Santa Monica, CA: Dennis-Landman.

Rosen, E. (1957) *Dance in Psychotherapy.* Columbia, NY: Columbia University.

Rossi, E. (ed.) (1980) *The Collected Papers of Milton H. Erickson on Hypnosis, Vols 1, 2, 3, and 4.* New York, NY: Irvington.

Rowe, C.E. and MacIsaac, D.S. (1995) *Empathic Attunement.* Northvale, NJ: Aronson.

Rubin, J. (1984) *The Art of Art Therapy.* New York, NY: Brunner.

Rubin, J. (1987) *Approaches to Art Therapy.* New York, NY: Brunner.

Rubin, J. (1999) *Art Therapy: An Introduction.* Palo Alto, CA: Brunner.

Samuels, A. (1985) *Jung and the Post-Jungians.* London: Routledge and Kegan Paul.

Satir, V. (1967) *Conjoint Family Therapy.* Palo Alto, CA: Science & Behavior Books.

Satir, V. (1972) *People Making.* Palo Alto, CA: Science & Behavior Books.

Satir, V. (1975) *Helping Families to Change.* New York, NY: Aronson.

Satir, V. (1976) *Making Contact.* Millbrae, CA: Celestial Arts.

Satir, V. (1983a) *Conjoint Family Therapy.* Palo Alto, CA: Science and Behavior Books.

Satir, V. (1983b) *Satir Step-by-Step.* Palo Alto, CA: Science and Behavior Books.

Satir, V. *et al.* (1991) *Say it Straight.* Palo Alto, CA: Science and Behavior Books.

Schaefer, C. (1994a) *Family Play Therapy.* Northvale, NJ: Aronson.

Schaefer, C. (1994b) *Handbook of Play Therapy.* New York, NY: Wiley.

Schatzman, M. (1971) Kingsley Hall: The politics of madness, Contemporary Psychoanalysis, 8: 107–21.

Schoop, T. (1974) *Won't You Join The Dance?* Palo Alto, CA: National.

Seashore, C.E. (1967) *The Psychology of Music.* New York, NY: Dover.

Shapiro, D.H. (1987) *Precision Nirvana.* Englewood Cliffs, NJ: Prentice.

Shapiro, F. (1995) *EMDR: Eye Movement Desensitization and Reprocessing.* New York, NY: Guilford Press.

Sherman, R. and Freeman, N. (1986) *Handbook of Structured Techniques in Marriage and Family Therapy.* New York, NY: Brunner/Mazel.

Spiegler, M.D. and Guevremont, D.C. (1998) *Contemporary Behavior Therapy,* 3rd edn. Pacific Grove, CA: Brooks/Cole.

Stahl, S.M. and Munter, N. (2000) *Essential Psychopharmacology.* New York, NY: Cambridge University Press.

St Clair, M. (2000) *Object Relations and Self Psychology.* Belmont, CA: Brooks/ Cole.

Stolorow, R.D., Brandchaft, B. and Atwood, G.E. (1987) *Psychoanalytic Treatment.* Hillsdale, NJ: Analytic Press.

Strachey, J. (1934) The nature of the therapeutic action of psychoanalysis, *International Journal of Psycho-Analysis,* 15: 127–59.

Thompson, R.A. (1996) *Counselling Techniques.* London: Taylor & Francis.

Van Kaam, A. (1966) *The Art of Existential Counseling.* Tempe, AZ: Dimension Books.

W, Bill (2000) *Bill W.: My First 40 Years.* netLibrary Inc.

Waden, H. (1980) *Art Psychotherapy.* New York, NY: Wiley.

Walsh, R. and Vaughan, F. (1993) *Paths Beyond Ego.* Los Angeles, CA: J.P. Tarcher.

Wastell, C.A. (1999) Defensive focus and the defense style questionnaire, *Journal of Nervous and Mental Disease*, 187: 217–23.

Watson, J.B. (1913) Psychology as the behaviorist views it. *Psychological Review*, 20: 158–77.

Watzlawick, P., Beavin, J. and Jackson, D. (1967) *Pragmatics of Human Communications*. New York, NY: W.W. Norton.

Whitaker, C. (1953) *The Roots of Psychotherapy*. New York, NY: Blakiston.

Whitaker, C. (1981) *The Roots of Psychotherapy*. New York, NY: Brunner/Mazel.

Whitaker, C. (1988) *Dancing with the Family*. New York, NY: Brunner-Mazel.

Whitaker, C. (1989) *Midnight Musing of a Family Therapist*. New York, NY: Norton.

Wilber, K. (1979) *No Boundary*. Boulder, CO: New Science/Shambhala.

Wilber, K. (1980) *The Atman Project*. Wheaton, IL: Quest.

Wilson, P.H., Spence, S.H. and Kavanagh, D.J. (1989) *Cognitive Behavioural Interviewing for Adults*. London: Routledge.

Winnicott, D.W.W. (1975) *Through Paediatrics to Psychoanalysis*. London: Karnac Books.

Wise, M. and Rundel, J. (1988) *Concise Guide to Consultation Psychiatry*. Washington, DC: American Psychiatric Press.

Wolpe, J. (1958) *Psychotherapy by Reciprocal Inhibition*. Stanford, CA: Stanford University Press.

Wolpe, J. (1981) Behavior therapy versus psychoanalysis: therapeutic and social implications, *American Psychologist*, 36: 159–64.

Wolpe, J. (1982) *The Practice of Behavior Therapy*, 3rd edn. New York, NY: Pergamon.

Wynne, L.C. *et al.* (1986) *Systems Consultation: A New Perspective for Family Therapy*. New York, NY: Guilford Press.

Zeig, J. (1982) *Ericksonian Approaches to Hypnosis and Psychotherapy*. New York, NY: Brunner/Mazel.

Zeig, J. (1992) *The Evolution of Psychotherapy: The Second Conference*. New York, NY: Brunner/Mazel.

Zeig, J. (1990) *What is Psychotherapy?: Contemporary Perspectives*. San Francisco, CA: Jossey-Bass.

Zuk, G.H. (1981) *Family Therapy: A Triadic-Based Approach*. Dordrecht, AZ: Kluwer Academic Publishers.

Zuk, G.H. (1986) *Process and Practice in Family Therapy*. Dordrecht, AZ: Kluwer Academic Publishers.

Index

INTERNALIZATION
THE ORIGINS AND CONSTRUCTION OF INTERNAL REALITY

Kenneth C. Wallis and James L. Poulton

The process of internalization is fundamental to all forms of psychotherapy. It is difficult to see how any healing process is meaningful unless the one to be healed 'takes home' some element of the cure. How else may a 'cure' take place unless it is *internalized*? This book surveys the development of concepts pertaining to the processes by which an individual's internal world comes into being. The core concepts of internalization – identification, incorporation and introjection, which heavily influenced the evolution of psychanalytic schools, illustrate the commonalities and differences between a wide variety of psychotherapeutic paradigms. Through an examination of representative proponents of the four major sub-divisions of psychotherapeutic schools – Psychoanalysis, Cognitive-Behavioural, Humanistic/Existential and Family-Systems – the authors show how internalizing concepts and principles shed light on the theory and practice of psychotherapy.

The universality of the human condition and the humanitarian goal of psychotherapeutic healing pose an ethical mandate to search for common threads of meaning across the paradigmatic spectrum. *Internalization* addresses that mandate through elucidation of concepts as applied to a variety of theoretical contexts. Through this comparative method, the authors hope to contribute to the self-examination of the psychotherapeutic enterprise, and to elucidate the mechanisms underlying therapeutic efficacy.

Contents
Core concepts of internalization – Internalization in psychoanalytic schools – Internalization in behaviourism and cognitive-behavioural schools – Internalization in family, systems and group schools – Internalization in humanistic/existential schools – The validity of internalization theory: thesis and antithesis – References – Index.

208pp   0 335 20305 1 (Paperback)   0 335 20306 X (Hardback)

THE THERAPEUTIC ENVIRONMENT
CORE CONDITIONS FOR FACILITATING THERAPY

Richard J. Hazler and Nick Barwick

Psychology bookshelves are filled with texts on different theories of how to do therapy and why one specific theory will work better than all the others. Yet the fact is research proves over and over again that *all* theories can work under the right conditions. This book takes a unique look at the specifics of those conditions that are facilitative to all forms of therapy, and how they are identified in different theories.

The diverse experiences and viewpoints of an American humanistic therapist and a British psychodynamic therapist are brought together to explore the essential conditions needed for therapy to succeed. Extensive use of first-hand examples and thorough academic support combine to create vivid text, a sound theoretical base and practical therapeutic applications. The opening chapters draw on substantial research evidence which suggests that all theoretical approaches are equally effective in the hands of good therapists. It proposes that an important factor contributing to this effectiveness is the environment in which therapy is practised. Three central chapters give in-depth explorations of the unique ways in which the broad theoretical orientations of Psychodynamic, Existential-Humanistic, and Cognitive-Behavioural deal with the philosophy, labelling, function, perspective and implementation of a facilitative environment. A concluding chapter synthesizes information from these diverse orientations to identify core commonalities and critical differences between how therapists from different theoretical persuasions develop common understandings, maintain working client relationships and regulate their personal involvement in therapy.

Contents

160pp   0 335 20282 9   (Paperback)   0 335 20283 7 (Hardback)

CHARACTER AND PERSONALITY TYPES

Nick Totton and Michael Jacobs

It is very difficult for the student or practitioner to find their way through the jungle of different personality typographies that has sprung up in the field of psychotherapy; and even harder for them to find a point of sufficient height above the forest canopy to get their bearings in order to compare one system with another. This volume offers such an observation point together with some possible mappings. It surveys how different schools of therapy approach a basic topic, the differences that exist between people – including their attitudes, feelings, concerns and talents. It examines different systematic and non-systematic approaches to identifying different types of human being, exploring whether there are systematic ways in which humans vary, how we can assess the merit of different typologies, and whether personality typing is a helpful approach to therapy.

Character and Personality Types looks in detail at the arguments for and against the use of typologies of character and personality as a clinical tool; and offers general criteria for judging the merits of particular personality systems, as well as exploring the possibility of a wider synthesis.

Contents
Orientations – Character in psychoanalysis – Reich and his heirs – Jungian typology – Humanistic and research based typologies – Transpersonal typologies – Conclusion – Further reading – References – Index.

160pp   0 335 20639 5 (Paperback)   0 335 20640 9 (Hardback)